CW00642776

# Call Me Tim

Julien Chilcott-Monk

**Dogberry Books**

ISBN (eBook): 978-1-7398164-6-9

ISBN (Paperback): 978-1-7398164-5-2

ISBN (Hardback): 978-1-7398164-8-3

www.dogberrybooks.com

www.julienchilcott-monk.com

*Also by Julien Chilcott-Monk*

A Calendar of Catholic Devotion

Come, Lord Jesus!

Flesh, Bone, Wood

A Basic Dictionary of Bible People

Walking the Way of the Cross

John Henry Newman and the Path to Sainthood

In the Name of the Father

The Nails and the Cross

Visions

Saints of the Roman Canon

The Way of the Passion

Advent Joy - Journeying towards the Nativity

Praying the Crucifix

Week by week with St John Henry Newman

A Catholic Companion

*To Neil,*
*who knows all these things better than most*

# Table of Contents

Foreword ..................................................................... 1

Introduction ................................................................. 3

My Friend Tim................................................................ 17

Tim the Historian ......................................................... 33

    The Mary Rose ....................................................... 33

    The Battlefields Trust ........................................... 53

    The Battle of Homildon Hill .................................. 61

    Towards Agincourt ............................................... 73

Tim the Actor ............................................................... 91

    Memories from the acting world............................ 91

    Churchill .............................................................. 105

    All Creatures Great and Small............................... 115

    Sense and Sensibility............................................ 124

    The Shooting Party............................................... 127

    Castles in the Air ................................................. 134

Tim and the Family ....................................................... 149

    Paul and Sarah ..................................................... 149

    Elizabeth ............................................................. 155

    Justine ................................................................ 161

    Emma .................................................................. 167

    Neil ..................................................................... 173

Tim and his Maker ........................................................ 183

Afterword ................................................................... 189

Chronology .................................................................. 195

Acknowledgments ........................................................ 203

# Foreword

Tim and I were certainly very fond of each other. After all, he was one of the most charming men I have ever known. He was the most hard-working of actors, and yet he had time to be an excellent bowyer, a splendid archer, and a most knowledgeable historian. More than that, he was the country's foremost expert on the longbow, a polished author, and a leading light in the Mary Rose Trust for forty years.

In his memory I have planted a yew tree, which was a sapling from the yew under which the Magna Carta was signed. We all miss him enormously.

Dame Judi Dench

# Introduction

This is not purely a biography, though there are many biographical details, it is true. Neither is it purely an appreciation of Robert Hardy's life's work as an actor, or indeed, as a bowyer, an historian, or as an author, even though all of this appears. Allow me to gather what I can from those who knew him well in all these different fields.

So, what about this book? Well, it is a collage, a mélange (more in the mixed bag sense than the ragbag sense), an omnium gatherum, indeed. Perhaps collage defines the book best as it will be the cumulative effect of each person's contribution, as it is made, that will gradually give us A Portrait of Robert Hardy.

Timothy Sydney Robert Hardy - Tim to his friends and relations - was often, but not always, seen rather differently by the fellow actor and by, say, a fellow historian or by a fellow bowyer and by a fellow author. As a trustee of the Mary Rose Trust, he might have appeared rather different from a trustee of the Battlefields Trust, and so on. I give, for example, my personal memoir, which you will largely find as the chapter My Friend Tim. In correspondence, I asked Carol Drinkwater to read my personal account and she conceded it pictured a side of Tim never revealed to her whilst acting in the early series of *All Creatures Great and Small.* She asserted that she had had a close acting relationship with Tim, and a social life as well. However, she saw little of the Tim I knew. This will be shown – to a greater or lesser degree – as we progress. But I believe all the basic building blocks of the Tim we all knew can be recognized in everyone's account – wit, generosity, and perfectionism. Of course, we all saw his strengths and his weaknesses. We all have both. For example, Tim's flash of ire, usually born of impatience, was often just that – a flash. The chin might jut out a little with the look of a ready pugilist from time to time, but verbal fisticuffs, I think, were rare. (If in doubt, one would change the subject or, if one was in an adventurous mood, one might goad a little.)

When you have read and pinned all the sketches to the evidence board, you will be able to step back and admire the result and make up your own mind as to how often he appeared differently to some, or if he preferred to keep one part of his life largely sealed from another. I have not yet quite made up my mind.

As an introduction to what lies ahead, let us look at four different memories of Tim from very different angles. Geoff Pope of the Tewkesbury Battlefield Society fires the starting cannon, revealing his Robert Hardy as a man of infinite patience:

'To commemorate Robert after his death, The Tewkesbury Battlefields Society organized the planting of a yew tree on the battlefield site, as Judi Dench did in her garden. Robert's daughter, Justine, attended the event, and gave a moving speech. Tim would open the festival year by year with a little Shakespeare and rousing words to get the battle started. He was Patron of the Medieval Festival Society, which gave rise to The Tewkesbury Battlefield Society. The Society arranges the annual battle re-enactment on the actual battlefields of Tewkesbury. Over two-thousand "re-enactors" from all over the world are involved each year and Tim never failed to impress his audiences at the side events that occurred throughout the festival weekend.

If not in a rush to return home, Tim often held court in the public bar of his hotel with residents and fascinated casual drinkers. Additionally, he helped with the Mayor of Tewkesbury's charity work by giving talks and little performances, which he thoroughly enjoyed as did his entirely captivated audiences. I had been warned that I might find the man 'feisty': I never found him so.'

*  *  *

In the introduction to the auctioneer's catalogue advertising the sale of those goods Tim was unable to take with him when he made his move to Avington, Tim was quoted: 'Downsizing, and losing a great part of a treasured library, make for sadness. Entrusting it to the auctioneers has taken much of the pain away, and through them and their careful work I wish anyone, who comes to possess anything that was mine, as much joy and pleasure as it has given me through the years.'

It was clearly the case that Colin Meays and his colleague had softened the blow of losing treasured possessions when they were asked to call at the Charlbury house to value antiquarian books, furniture, and other items:

'As is often the case when you are in a hurry to arrive on time, we were delayed. As my colleague drove, I telephoned Mr Hardy a little nervously but assumed a secretary would answer. To my surprise the telephone was answered with a Hardy 'Hello!' travelling down to the earpiece making me feel as though I were on the set of *All Creatures Great and Small*. Directions given and we continued the journey without ado. We were ushered into the kitchen where coffee and biscuits awaited us. 'I am an actor,' he confessed unnecessarily, as he showed us the library we were to examine.

Robert sang at the top of his voice as he moved about the house. After a little while our host suggested he play some Praetorius for me, which he did at full volume. That over, he switched to Sibelius for my colleague. Again, the volume knob was thrust round to its fullest extent. The volume was tremendous; listing the books on a Dictaphone was not made any easier. A gin and tonic finished the day. We were asked to return to continue our assessments, which we did on a number of occasions, the days being broken nicely by pub lunches. The resulting auction took place in April 2015, and I collected Tim for a private viewing. His daughter, Justine, and his secretary Neil joined us. Tim was in splendid spirits, given that this must have been a very hard time for him.'

I know that Tim was very grateful for Colin's softening the blow of seeing his comforting 'stuff' disappear in such large quantities. Colin was certainly 'starstruck' by Tim, who rather rewarded him by having a special way of addressing him. 'Cole – in' would always be his pronunciation, not because he otherwise pronounced the name in that way, but simply because he thought it would seem special to Colin. (This was a trait of Tim's. We shall come to the actor, James Murray, in a chapter or two but it might be worth mentioning that Tim would always refer to James's young daughter as though her name, Nell, was a diminutive of Nelson. 'Must be difficult for you, James, not knowing when your daughter will be called away on the high seas.' Tim simply loved this sort of nonsense.)

***

Giovanna Cresswell-Forrester established and maintains the online Robert Hardy Fan Club and her love of Tim and her fascination for his work and the personality he projected became almost an obsession when still a teenager and growing up.

'I first met Robert Hardy in April 1973 when I was visiting HMS Victory with my mother. I was twelve years old, but already I 'knew' him from *Manhunt* and *Elizabeth R.* Mum had been a fan for much longer and I was aware from the glint in her eye that we were going to say 'hello' to him, come what may. Robert was on a private tour of the ship along with his wife, Sally, and their two young daughters. At the spot where Admiral Lord Nelson had fallen, fatally wounded, my mother struck up an abstract conversation with the great actor. I remember talk of British Sovereignty, the Common Market, and the dearth of decent national heroes, like Nelson, God bless him. [At about this time Edward Heath had squeezed us into the Common Market. Tim was no friend of that organization or its subsequent aliases.] It was a well-chosen approach, engaging Tim enthusiastically. We three children greeted one another politely and then continued by shooting each other sideward glances of the type that can only be produced by young girls in an awkward situation. My mother introduced me to Tim. Thankfully, I suppressed a sudden urge to curtsey, because when he looked at me, I was mesmerized. He was ravishing! I had no idea the impact this striking gentleman would have on my life.'

Sadly, Giovanna's mother died not long after this encounter. She was grief-stricken at the loss of her mother. Some comfort came when she was reminded of the effect the HMS Victory meeting had had upon her when watching Edward VII. Her devotion to the actor was rekindled, and then came *All Creatures Great and Small*. She felt herself urged to find out as much as possible about this man and scoured press cuttings, news bulletins, magazine articles and so forth, in order to build up a proper picture of him. (I seem to remember my sister doing similar research on her favourite actor of the time, Dirk Bogarde.)

It is interesting to note how *All Creatures Great and Small* took hold of people. It was extremely popular. However, although Tim was fairly satisfied with most of it, he was slightly frustrated when that was all they could talk about. 'I've done so many worthier performances, weightier performances' he complained once 'why don't they remember those.' I assured him that *Henry V* and *The Wilderness Years* were still etched in most people's memories but to remember he did make dozens of episodes of the vet series. He accepted that but was once very cross with me for having a poster designed with 'ROBERT HARDY (Siegfried in *All Creatures Great and Small*)' plastered over it. I learnt my lesson.

So, returning to the theme in hand, Giovanna faithfully amassed a vast archive of Hardy history, which was good therapy for her still suffering as she was from the premature death of her mother. When Giovanna, as an adult, finally met Tim – by that time she had been trained as and had become a psychologist - she was able to admit her somewhat obsessive behaviour. However, all the work she put into the project equipped her to build the Robert Hardy Fan Club site.

'In 2012, I established the 'Robert Hardy Fan Club' on the internet. I was now ready to share my fondness of Robert with other people. The fan club attracted folk from all over the planet, each one with their own Robert Hardy story. I was amazed at the number of people who said he had touched their lives in a lasting and personal way. It wasn't just me then! Here was an actor with an extraordinary ability to affect his audience – and reach much deeper than the superficial level of a performance. I decided I had to let him know and thank him, on behalf of all his fans. I expounded my story with humour, deciding that if I was to be written off as a 'nutter' I might as well be seen as a funny one. Wonderfully, Robert became the avuncular friend I always craved. I amused him. He teased me 'I am glad to have been of service to you for all those years, but I cannot begin to comprehend why you chose me'. I went from a fan to a friend. He went from Robert to Tim. He loved a bout of teasing and I adored making him chuckle. That laugh…anyone who has heard it will know what I mean.

At Avington fete in June 2016, he granted me 'access all areas' telling me I was welcome to be anywhere he was. And I was finally getting answers to all my questions, but each answer only generated twenty new questions. With a raised eyebrow and that familiar chuckle, he said, 'Giovanna, I'll either answer all your questions or I'll die first.' I thought that worthy of a reproach and tapped him on the knee. It was just bone. His arms too. 'I'm eating well' he said. That only made it more obvious. Time was in no mood to be patient. In 2015 I had written to the Cabinet Office and nominated Tim for KBE. A Knighthood seemed the obvious reward. With Tim's daughters' guidance and Neil's, we agreed to keep the nomination campaign from him and after I saw him for the last time, about Easter 2017, I contacted the Cabinet Office again to tell them that there was little time left. I was assured 'Robert Hardy is under active consideration for a Knighthood."

Giovanna gives statistics of the Fan Club. At its height, it attracted ten-and-a-half thousand members. There were, it seems, more men than women (surprising!) and more members from the *All Creatures Great and Small* generation and thus fewer from the *Harry Potter* generation. Members hailed from the Philippines, Mexico, Norway, and South Africa. Indeed, every corner of the world. However, the United States provided the greatest contribution in terms of members, apart, of course, from the United Kingdom. Numbers from Australia were small but from New Zealand, the numbers were more significant.

***

I later mention only briefly Tim's connection with the Royal Armouries, but here we ought to include Guy Wilson's account of Tim's involvement in the transfer of the museum from the Tower of London. It reveals, or *emphasizes*, Tim's dogged determination, his bloodhound dedication to seeing a project through to its conclusion. (Guy was one time Master of the Armouries.)

'Tim served as a trustee of the Royal Armouries from 1983 to 1994. He was always a very popular trustee with staff, not because he was a famous and great actor but because he always had time for them and was genuinely interested in their lives and ideas. He served at a time of great change in the museum which saw it expand from the Tower of London on to two other sites – the artillery museum at Fort Nelson, near Portsmouth and then, far more controversially, the new main museum in Leeds. He was a staunch supporter of the plan to move the bulk of the museum and its staff from the Tower of London and helped enormously both with public relations and with the design of the new museum and its displays.

In 1994 at the topping-out ceremony of the new museum, Tim shot a whistling arrow from the roof as part of a pageant of arms through the ages. And in 1996 at the Royal Opening, Tim reprised his role as Winston Churchill in the

Masque that was performed before Her Majesty the Queen. All in all, he gave considerable amounts of time to the museum, including helping to make several promotional films. I remember one occasion when Tim had agreed to do some pieces to camera in the Tower about the history of the Armouries within that royal fortress. I offered to send him some briefing notes to help him prepare. 'No,' came the reply, 'just buy me lunch beforehand and we'll talk about it then.' So, at midday on the day of the shoot, Tim arrived at the Tower, and we enjoyed lunch in the Tower Hotel. Eventually, the conversation drifted round to the afternoon's work. I sketched the areas or work left for Tim to cover. Tim took a few notes on a piece of paper certainly no larger than an opened-out cigarette packet! Then we returned to earlier topics until 2 o'clock, the designated time for the first piece to camera on the Wall Walk. We arrived just in time. Tim greeted the crew and was allotted his position. He took a quick glance at his notes and proceeded to complete a flawless piece at first take. And so it continued for the rest of the afternoon. No second takes were necessary. Tim was a true master of his craft.'

***

Michael Linnit was Tim's agent for fifty-three years; indeed, for most of Tim's career. Michael was his trusted and beloved friend, and the relationship was a good, happy, and fruitful one. It certainly stood the test of time. It was a great pity that Michael was unable to attend Tim's memorial service on St Crispin's Day (Agincourt Day) 25th October 2017, but he entrusted the following words to the actor, Peter Davison, who delivered them with aplomb. Asking permission of Michael to use these words, he willingly gave me his 'unreserved consent'. And I think they set us on our journey very well indeed…

'Timbo! – handsome, dashing, charming, immensely trim and athletic, complex, demanding, exacting, difficult, irascible, gifted and with the most magical redeeming sense of humour. Virtually every conversation we had over fifty-three years had an element of humour. I always carried a determination, of which Timbo was aware, to deflate any pomposity he may have been displaying. I knew I had won when his seriousness collapsed into uncontrollable laughter. Timbo! - How blessed we are to have known you. God bless you and God's speed.'

# My Friend Tim

I am, of course, only one of a large number of those who can claim to have enjoyed the close acquaintance of the late Robert Hardy – Tim to his friends and relations – that fine, classical actor, historian, author, raconteur and wit. And I can make such a claim only in respect of the last dozen years or so of his long and fruitful life.

I first met Tim, a friend of the Montagu family, at Beaulieu Abbey where he was narrating the history of the dissolved Cistercian Monastery and the subsequent Beaulieu Palace, as part of an evening's entertainment taking place in the parish church – the former refectory of the monastery. (According to Ralph, the present Baron, Tim and his father had become friends when Tim was involved in a festival of the English longbow taking place in the grounds of Beaulieu Palace, for the delectation of the visitors, holidaymakers and aficionados.) During the evening and the narration, there was a succession of courses of a 'frugal' monastic meal served to the audience spiced by suitable choral music of the period supplied by my choir, Vox Humana. This enabled the narrator to catch his breath.

It was a fairly lengthy affair. The audience was presented with nettle soup, devilled wild mushrooms, bread and cheese; you know the sort of thing. The music? I think I gave them a little Gregorian chant, a few French motets, and some English Renaissance pieces.

Anxious to meet the man, I climbed the well-worn stone steps to the reader's pulpit within the refectory wall - one of the very few such pulpits remaining in England - at the conclusion of the evening.

'I thought I'd pop over from the gallery as we have worked together this evening without ever having met.'

'My script was far too long.'

'You read it very well.' I remember how crass that sounded.

'That's hardly the point.' He collected his papers from the reading desk saying, 'Your pieces were short.'

'Too short?'

'Probably.'

I changed the subject slightly. 'Would you care to be photographed with my choir? They' d like it.'

'Of course.'

We descended the precarious steps gingerly.

'I don't know if you would be interested in doing something with the choir sometime. I have a script I am working on. The character is a witty old shepherd, the narrator in my adaptation of a twelfth century liturgical drama. His name is Tom.'

'Send it to me. I shall have a look and let you know what I think.'

Knowing his reputation for dismissing poor scripts with disdain, I suddenly felt like a small boy rather overenthusiastic about the essay he was handing in.

'I remember you as Pontius Pilate in Dennis Potter's *Son of Man*, sometime in the 1960s.' I thought I'd fill in any silence but I felt an unseen glare in the gloom of the Abbey. 'From Dennis to Harry.' The attempt at such a pun or wisecrack, or whatever it was, was, mercifully, ignored.

'Oh, I'd been in the business of well over twenty years by then.'

So, from this rather stiff, unpromising, and awkward beginning, our relationship developed. But he was indeed photographed with the choir and, to the frustration of the photographer, fell into deep conversation with one of my sopranos, who seemed to have a tenuous, neighbourly connection with one of his sisters-in-law.

A week or so later, I sent the script based on one I had written in the 1980s. I had rewritten it with what I knew, or thought I knew, about Tim, hoping to delight him with the wittiness of the piece. But I was not going to count my chickens. It was, therefore, a happy surprise to hear him on the telephone only some three days later. 'Yes, I have the script. I love it. Great fun! I'll be a Dorset shepherd.' He gave me the last sentence in an authentic Dorsetshire burr.

'Splendid, may I buy you lunch; we can discuss it further, then?'

'You can find Oxford well enough, of course.' He then proceeded to give meticulous directions from Oxford to his Charlbury house. Telephone kiosks, traffic cameras, pillar boxes, restaurants, garages, even jewellers and odd turnings, obscure features and obvious landmarks were all identified and dictated to me. 'Now, have you got all that?'

'I think so.'

'I hope so.'

I arrived at eleven at what always seemed to me a large early nineteenth century vicarage, ready to discuss the project, then lunch. Tim's godson and P.A. - Neil Nisbet, actor, co-director of a children's theatre school and art restorer – responded to the bell. As I said 'Chilcott-Monk to see Mr Hardy' Neil's face clouded slightly.

'Is he expecting you?'

'I hope so; we agreed the arrangements over the telephone last week.'

I noticed a fox mask and brush hanging from the newel post as I was shown into the viewing room with large television and hampers of videotapes and DVDs, and an empty dog basket. I was given coffee. Clearly, my leading actor was still in bed, perhaps dealing with correspondence or reading the newspaper.

I could hear Radio 3 broadcasting dimly. All this descended the main staircase.

'Fetch my diary, would you? Thanks. How did this happen? Here, look…Chilcott-Monk, 11 o'clock – script consultation, lunch… But it's been scrubbed. BBC this afternoon at 4. Oh Hell! The BBC rang to postpone. I've scrubbed the wrong one.' All this was distinct, but in a much larger voice, a stage voice, he boomed for my benefit, 'So sorry, I'll be down in about an hour. So sorry!'

The window was suddenly opened by someone outside and the rude face of a white-coated man grinned at me and winked. 'All right, mate? Nice mornin' for it!' I agreed. He began to paint. Thus, I was entertained until the great actor made his descent. 'I am very sorry. Quite inexcusable. I can't think what happened. No, that's untrue, I know precisely what happened.'

'Think nothing of it.'

Tim drove us to lunch in his ancient but immaculate BMW, registration, for some reason or other, RH 666.

'I shall lead the way' he said at the threshold of the pub with its Michelin Star chef, and strode away through the entrance and between the tables of patrons, lunching in twos and threes.

As I followed, I overheard two women talking quietly in loud voices to one another. 'That's Robert Hardy, the actor, and I think I know the older one behind him.'

Now I soon learned that I did indeed share much in common with Tim such as a difficulty with and a distrust of arithmetic – in boyhood, anyway – and in that our fathers had both been schoolmasters. But one thing I did not share with him was my age, being some twenty years his junior! Of course, until his last months, Tim rarely looked anywhere near his age.

We talked of the script and the intended production. I heard his impression of Elizabeth Taylor whom he regarded, I think, with little warmth largely on account of her hold over his friend since Magdalen College, Richard Burton. He admired Gielgud's acting. (Tim had been Ariel to Gielgud's Prospero at Stratford in the fifties.) He told me how, in more modern times, he had admired the young Peter Davison when he was cast as his younger brother in *All Creatures Great and Small*. There were many witty reminiscences, not least that he had been tutored by both C. S. Lewis and J. R. R. Tolkien. (I do believe he became more involved with Lewis and Tolkien every time he touched on this period of his life.) He grinned impishly as he admitted his academic achievement of 'a scruffy Third. I could write a good essay but otherwise…' Tim related in great detail the story of the terrifying coach crash that occurred during the filming of *The Shooting Party*, which we shall revisit later.

'What was that?' I asked innocently.

'You don't know the film?'

'Not at all, I'm afraid.'

'Really?' He stared at me wide-eyed in mock astonishment.

We talked of animals and his love of horses. We talked of dogs, more especially, his current pet, Crécy, a whippet, a distant and remote cousin of Christie, one of the gang of dogs that habitually spilled from Siegfried Farnon's car in that well-known television series. I told him I preferred Cocker spaniels.

'Oh, no, they're daft.'

'True, but that's precisely why I like them.'

'No, I've seen Crécy take down a muntjac: that's the sort of man he is.'

I had, in fact, caught sight of the dog that morning, quivering on the first landing. 'Why didn't he come down to meet me?'

'He's afraid of the smell of fresh paint.'

We also found time for Tom the Shepherd.

I visited again the following month with the full score of my adaptation of the Nativity drama *The Play of Herod*. Again, he tried his efficient Dorset burr (always better after gin) never ever sounding like stagey mummerset. At the time there was a little difficulty – particularly in his drawing room – with mice. They would pinch the fringes of the fine rugs for their nests in the wall behind one of the two fireplaces in the room. That morning, however, some success again had been achieved through the medium of the mousetrap. Suddenly Tim began an hilarious little monologue in the brogue he had earmarked for Tom the Shepherd.

'Poor ol' Ruthy bought it last noight, an' that makes four of us now, all gone. Gone, I'll 'low, to the great mouse'ole in the sky, cut in 'alf by the spring of that-there trap gadget. Uncle Jasper las' week, gone; 'is strange young son, Cuthert too. An', course, there was 'is sister, 'Arriet, with the squint. She jus' couldn't see the trap, I s'pose, looking the other way, sort of – as she alwus did, on account of her squint like. An' now poor ol' Ruthy.'

We met again shortly afterwards to take some photographs for the posters and the programme. Tim, dressed in his *All Creatures Great and Small* brown stock coat, cap and crook, posed in various attitudes with a flock of sheep in the background. He kept up a chatty Dorset throughout. To grab

25

his attention, I cautioned him in what I took to be a cheery Cockney accent. ''Ere, 'Ardy, if you don't shut your cake 'ole, I'll never get these bleedin' pictures took!' He grinned, his eyes sparkling with mischief.

At lunch that day, Tim took up my Cockney challenge and asked me, ''Ere, Matey, what d'you fancy from this menu? I mean it's all good scoff, ain't it?' From that moment we should, at the drop of a hat, lapse into a dialogue of nonsense, sometimes unable to extract ourselves, even when the waitresses came. Occasionally, a couple at the nearby table would move 'nearer the window, for the light, you know.'

''Ere, d'you fink e's done time?'

'What, that bloke over there? Yeah, probably.'

'Murder, I reckon.'

'Yeah, could be. Looks shifty enough. I blame the Labour Party, personally.'

'Well, yeah, of course, 'o wouldn't?'

Resuming our normal selves, I declared that I should have made a rather good bad actor.

'Don't be modest, you are already.'

Tim gave his Tom the Shepherd performance twice, once at the Oratory in Oxford and once in Romsey Abbey. Critics warmed to his accent, his sense of fun and the extraordinarily accurate camel roar he tried at the Oratory but not in the Abbey. After the first performance, he telephoned, ''Ere, you done my froat in!' By now he had completed his final Harry Potter film and had signed to record an episode of Lewis (*Dark Matters*) in which he was to play an Oxford Professor of music.

When we next met, Tim told me with much glee that as he stepped up to conduct a movement from *The Planets*, the director had asked him if he would not prefer to use a baton. '"No, no," I said, "I shall conduct without a baton and adopt the method employed by my good friend the famous composer Julien Chilcott-Monk!"' He made strange clawing movements in the air.

'Did you really say that?' I asked. 'Anyway, I am not in the least famous.'

'No, I know. I thought you needed a filip.'

'Neither do I conduct like that.'

'Yes, you do.'

Soon Tim was studying a script I had given him for the role of Br. Joseph, a contemporary of St Hildegard of Bingen. When running through the part, he spoke with a German accent adjusting it as he went. 'I was well schooled for my Prince Albert accent.' Halfway through, he was in pure Siegfried Farnon mode

27

and anything but German. 'O Hell!' he exclaimed, 'I'm supposed to be bloody German. Direct me, direct me!' He resumed in his impeccable Prince Albert.

I had written a book about John Henry Newman to coincide with Pope Benedict's visit to this country and I used Newman's great poem *The Dream of Gerontius* as the framework of the book. It struck me how the poem might make a splendid sacred melodrama, mostly sung but with actors in the roles of the Angel and Gerontius using the spoken word. Clearly, this would be no competition for Elgar's sublime oratorio, but it would allow the text to be better heard and, perhaps, understood. Tim seemed keen on the idea when I produced a draft 'treatment' and persuaded Neil to be responsible for the part of the Angel.

After one of our usual lunches, I photographed the two of them in costume in the Charlbury drawing room. The first performance of Gerontius would take place at Beaulieu Abbey. As I snapped amateurishly, an articulated lorry reversed into the grounds of the house and came to rest beside the drawing room windows. Neil immediately swept out – he was dressed in an alb and white cincture – to tackle the lorry-driver and send him on his way. Tim began to snigger uncontrollably. 'Can you…(snort)…imagine the conversation…(snort)…back at the depot? "'Ere, you lot, I buggered up where I was an' reversed into this geyser's grounds an' suddenly this bloody priest comes runnin' out the house an' tells me to sling my 'ook! A bloody priest!'" We were enmeshed in a cockney conversation when Neil returned. However, I could not resume the photography and try to snap a supposedly dying Gerontius who would not stop giggling.

We performed this sacred melodrama four times over the next few years. At Beaulieu, it was done with a small ensemble and little percussion. Ralph Montagu (then the heir to the Barony) enjoyed it enough to see the Christchurch Cathedral performance in Oxford where it was performed with larger forces. Afterwards we dined and much shocked or surprised Ralph's wife (and mine) with our inevitable double act.

The final performance of *Gerontius* occurred in Winchester Cathedral but the third was given in the Oxford Oratory, where it was recorded. And it is a precious recording because Tim brilliantly explored in depth all the emotions in which the dying man and then the soul was caught. It was a remarkable and splendid performance and I treasure it. After four performances, Tim felt that he was getting too close to his own death-bed even though that was still a few years away.

Throughout this time, Tim appeared on television as Willy Whitelaw, Tite Barnacle Snr. and once again as his beloved Churchill. The many other facets of his life included, as we all know, the longbow, the Mary Rose, and the battlefields of England, about which he had an encyclopaedic knowledge, and all about which we shall hear more. Often when driving in Hampshire and Berkshire, I'd be asked 'When was the famous battle in that field?' Rarely did I know. Once or twice, I remember paying the penalty for suggesting that the longbow arrows were 'fired'. 'You shoot them; you don't fire them!' And a little later I thought I had fallen into the same trap. Tim was now living at Avington Park, near Winchester. He was in the adjacent kitchen, and I spoke softly to Neil. 'I mentioned firing an arrow again the other day but I think I got away with it.' We grinned at each other. 'No, you bloody well didn't,' boomed the Hardy tones immediately.

When Lord (Edward) Montagu died, Tim telephoned. 'Are you attending the funeral?'

'Yes, of course.'

'Can you give me a lift?'

'Of course.'

'What are you wearing?'

'At this moment? Gardening clothes.'

'To the funeral! They'll be dressed formally, you know.'

'Do you think so?'

'Of course! I shall wear tails and topper.'

'Frock coat and black cravat all right?'

'Perfect, I should say.'

We were, of course, unique, save for one old uncle of the family, in our black clothing, among the casual, relaxed, short-skirted and be-jeaned!

Tim remained busy throughout the last few years and made a memorable appearance in Winchester's Theatre Royal discussing with the actor, James Murray, his remarkable performance as Churchill in BBC's *The Wilderness Years*. But by the time he held his drinks party just before Christmastide in 2016, he had already begun to feel that he was shutting down. He declined steadily and we neither lunched nor dined again but corresponded by letter and telephone. He often sought clarification of something I had written either in a book or in a letter. I remember that Transubstantiation was one of our last topics. He died – and he would think this great fun – on my birthday, surrounded by his children and his Godson, Neil. Even in his sorrow, Neil could not separate the scene in his mind from the rehearsals and performances of *Gerontius*.

On one occasion, Tim had my choir, Neil and me in fits of laughter when he called me over, in mid-rehearsal, as he pointed to the frontispiece of his score to which I had attached a portrait of John Henry Newman in characteristic pose with left elbow resting and left hand against his ear.

'Look, he's using what must have been the very first mobile 'phone. Did you know that?'

'You called me over for that?'

'But it's very funny.'

Everyone thought so. Happily, that very moment was captured on camera.

'Angels to whom the willing task is given, shall tend and nurse, and lull thee, as thou liest: and Masses on earth, and prayers in heaven, shall aid thee at the throne of Most Highest. Farewell, but not for ever! And I will come and wake thee on the morrow.' (*The Dream of Gerontius* – Saint John Henry Newman)

# Tim the Historian

## The Mary Rose

### Sank in 1545, Raised in 1982

A hundred-and-forty-eight feet long, keeled in elm but largely built of English oak in around 1510. The Mary Rose may well have been upgraded a number of times and certainly in 1536 her tonnage was nearly doubled, and her armoury brought up to date with the very latest iron and bronze cannon and many lighter, swivel guns. She sank with hundreds of archers, gunners, and other crew: very few men survived.

I visited Nick Rule, the son of the late Margaret Rule, the driving force and motivator behind the remarkable recovery of the Tudor warship, the Mary Rose. I was anxious to discover as much as I could about Tim's involvement. To give me a flavour of what I was after, Nick had generously assembled Terri Palmer, Margaret's personal assistant; the principal of the diving team; and John Selwyn Gilbert, the man who was responsible for the BBC's praiseworthy Mary Rose documentaries. Let's place him more precisely.

John Selwyn Gilbert filmed the Mary Rose excavation between 1980 and 1983. He made 114 working dives on the wreck with his underwater cameraman, Tim Johnson. Their first 'BBC Chronicle' film about the Mary Rose gained an award from the British Association for the Advancement of Science. Two other 'Chronicle' films followed. John Selwyn Gilbert produced and presented the Outside Broadcast when the Mary Rose was raised on 11th October 1982. The programme was nominated for a BAFTA award and was watched by more than 20 million people. In many respects the raising of this ship and, first, the meticulous excavation in the Solent silt and then the extraction of cannon and thousands of other important artefacts, changed, enlightened and informed many of the preconceived ideas we had about warfare in the sixteenth century and, indeed, sixteenth century life itself. For in that seemingly endless treasury of finds, many unique to modern eyes, were, inter alia, folk fiddles and three-holed tabor pipes, leather jerkins and footwear, caps, board games, dice and a domino, some barber-surgeon's equipment I have no wish to contemplate, and a leather pilgrim's wallet with the sacred letters IHS upon it. (These are the first three letters of the holy name, Jesus, in Greek – capitals Iota, Eta and Sigma.) And further joy – particularly to any bowyer, bowman, toxophilite, historian – there was found what appeared to be a longbow and then, sometime later, complete cases of longbows in splendid condition and many, many arrows. Up to that point only one miserable example of a longbow was known to exist, so most of the knowledge about the English longbow had been developed from experiment, contemporary drawings and sketches, educated surmise, and descriptions from various sources, some reliable, others not. It was Tim's dogged and painstaking research, encouraged by and born of his deeply-felt respect for Henry V, the monarch, and the man, that enabled him to produce, in 1976, his notable volume, *The Longbow – A social and military history.*

That Margaret was able to co-ordinate these excavations and encourage skilled engineers to come up with a method of raising what was remaining of the hull, is a great tribute to her. She was, of course, supported by HRH the Prince of Wales, and an ever-increasing team – from fundraisers to volunteers, from professors to dedicated amateurs. John Selwyn Gilbert kindly jotted down his view of how Tim fitted so well into this venture:

'Margaret Rule was Director of Archaeology at the Mary Rose Trust when the ship was raised, and she turned out to be an absolute genius at getting clever people to come and help. And one of the most interesting people she recruited was Tim Hardy, a great and famous actor, of course, but it was his enthusiasm for and knowledge of the longbow that brought him into Margaret's team, and he relished it enormously. First, he could at last get a look at the real thing. There were virtually no examples of original longbows before the Mary Rose was found. In the Tower of London there was a desiccated and misleading example. Longbows were not conserved when they were superseded by crossbows, muskets, and other weapons. They made excellent firewood! But longbows were still weapons of war, in active service, at the time the ship sank in 1545. And so, there were boxes and boxes of well-preserved longbows in the hold of the Mary Rose. There were longbows beside the skeletons of the dead archers on the main deck. It was extraordinary, quite extraordinary. Tim learned from everything that was found and it fired him up. Tim's personal competence with longbows was unrivalled - how to string them, handle them, and so on. The finer details of the longbow and its vital statistics were well known to him. His knowledge was unrivalled. The Mary Rose bows were designed for the use of young men who had practised the art every Sunday after church for years and years, since they were six or seven years old. As Tim would tell you, that is how the English archers and their arms won at Agincourt, Poitiers, and Crécy. Only a few modern archers can draw such formidably powerful bows.'

John also gives us a sense of what having Tim with them meant to the divers and support staff. Not only was he brimming with knowledge and capable of helping physically and intellectually, his very presence was a joy and inspiration. Tim was popular with the Mary Rose divers, partly because of his celebrity, but primarily because he was such an enthusiast. With Tim on the deck of the dive support vessel, stringing a replica bow, no one could fail to respond to his genuine excitement about the subjects of his study. Even the most exhausted young archaeologist, worn out and shaking with cold after an hour or more under water in the Solent silts, responded to the fun that would be engendered by having him on the team. And in his own environment, Tim's charm and generous nature put even the nervous and apprehensive at ease.

Naturally a shy person, Terri Palmer recalls that she was rather overawed to be entrusted by Margaret to deliver to Tim to store and test a consignment of the Mary Rose bows to his home at Upper Bolney, near Henley-on-Thames. He had devised special accommodation for the bows in the cellar. Terri was accompanied by her son, Jason, who was eleven years old at the time.

'I was a little scared at the idea of going to Robert Hardy's house and being entrusted with these ancient longbows. However, I should not have worried in the least because, naturally, he made us very welcome. We placed the longbows carefully and almost lovingly in the place he had made ready for them. He told me he was proud to be given the opportunity to study and 'to play with them'. During the weekend Tim produced a bow for each of us and we were thus introduced to archery – at a very basic level – which Jason loved. Alas, my aim was not so good!'

**\*\*\***

For over forty years Alex Hildred (BA, DSc, MCIFA, FSA) has worked at the Mary Rose Trust. She is Head of Research and Curator of Ordnance and Human Remains; from 1979 – 1982 Alex was a supervisor of the excavations. She willingly agreed to add to the story of Tim's involvement.

'The Mary Rose and Robert Hardy first came into contact in 1979. On 31st July, we were excavating the upper deck between the castles at each end of the ship when a stave was discovered, six feet long and in the shape of a 'D' in the centre, tapered to points at either end. It was different to anything we had found before. Margaret, the archaeological director, having amassed books covering the types of objects expected, already had a copy of *Longbow*. As was her wont she telephoned for advice and spoke to Robert. He was already working with John Levy and Peter Pratt. Together, they were investigating the capabilities of the great medieval longbow.

Then came the discoveries of the cases of longbows, individual longbows and all those arrows, along with a huge haul of other fascinating artefacts. Soon after recovery from the Solent, these bows were handed over to Robert to reside in specially constructed racks in his wine cellar. Here they were meticulously recorded, conserved and diligently weighed and wiped daily as they dried. When he left his Upper Bolney home for his Scottish castle, the bows were ready to be returned. However, this almost mystical union between man and bow, as with the archers of old endured until his death.

Why was this work so important historically? The only tangible evidence of the great warbows used at Agincourt and elsewhere are those from the Mary Rose, found together with over 2,000 arrows. Detailed recording, combined with an understanding of the behavioural characteristics of the yew wood under stress, enabled predictions regarding distance and impact. Ensuing trials with reproduction Mary Rose bows, shot by Simon Stanley, recording launch velocity, angle, and distance, have demonstrated their awesome power. This has transformed our understanding - and this is by no means an exaggeration – of their capability and the role and importance of archery within the battlefield context. Robert was instrumental in all of this.'

With these discoveries, Tim had updated his book, *Longbow*, in a fresh edition and he went on to write with Matthew Strickland, Professor of Medieval History at Glasgow University, *The Great Warbow – from Hastings to the Mary Rose*. The definitive tome, indeed. We shall hear from Matthew elsewhere, but he felt obliged to apologize for the delay in publication (2005). Alex Hildred records the reason…

'Matthew attributes the fact that the book was long in the making simply because Matthew and Robert had enjoyed their 'working dinners' far too much to bring the book to an end! From the moment first contact was made, Robert 'gave' to the Mary Rose Trust. A trustee for many years, he imbued the project not only with his scholarship, but with a guaranteed public profile – from gallery openings to gala evenings. At the museum opening in 2013, he joined us at Southsea Castle recounting the role of the archer to the media, as archers shot fire arrows towards the wreck site. When we revealed the final version of the Mary Rose Museum in July 2016, in spite of waning strength, Robert had recorded the 'voice over' for the 'big reveal' of the ship and was there on the day to celebrate with us.

I could not have completed the Mary Rose publication on the weapons of war without Robert's guidance, succour, support, contacts, and essays. That is a personal note, of course, but Robert is consistently described as a man of deep scholarship, who shared his passion and knowledge generously. Charming, eloquent, courteous, and witty, he brought stardust to every project that he was involved in and enchanted all those he worked with.'

Rear Admiral John Lippiett CB CBE DL, retired from the Royal Navy in 2003 to become Chief Executive of the Mary Rose Trust. For nearly thirteen years he threw his weight behind this fascinating project, which now sees an increasing number of enthusiastic visitors year after year. The ship, and the recovered artefacts, are now safely housed, as we have seen, in the perfect setting of the museum. (In order to give a little background, John was second-in-command of the frigate HMS Ambuscade during the Falklands War, and later commanded the frigate HMS Amazon, and the 9th Frigate Squadron and HMS Norfolk. John served as Rear Admiral, Chief of Staff to NATO Forces and, finally, Commandant of the Joint Service Command and Staff College. He now enjoys life as a lecturer and speaker to a great variety of bodies on old maps, exploration, and maritime history generally.) John kindly supplied me with the following memories of Tim.

'Arriving in 2003 at the Mary Rose Trust to take the helm of Henry VIII's flagship with the aim of completing the conservation of both the hull and the extraordinary collection of artefacts from within her, I met Dr Robert Hardy when hosting an event to celebrate the twenty-first anniversary of the memorable raising of the ship. He was our prime guest and gave the most wonderful talk on the longbow, displaying his deep knowledge of the weapon and its central place in the history of our great nation. We hit it off that day, and from that day until his death, we were in regular touch through telephone calls, letters, and visits. As my life became immersed in the challenge to save the ship and build a new museum, he remained at my side as a most able adviser, sage – and I feel privileged to say – a wonderful friend.

I came to realize that Tim's early work in studying the great longbow was concurrent with those pioneers of maritime exploration and excavation searching for the warship lost in battle off Portsmouth Harbour in 1545. While he was making his name on television, and in books about Agincourt and the longbow, divers were probing the thick mud of the Solent, eventually finding timbers, and then later recovering other objects from the seabed. Margaret Rule made first contact by telephone on the last day of July 1979.

With Tim as a central figure, the research into the bows recovered, after scientific tests and trials, rewrote history. Their power exceeded all previous estimates, transforming our understanding of their capabilities and the role and importance of archery in the battlefield. Tim's later book *The Great Warbow* which was written with Prof. Matthew Strickland, provided the definitive tome on the subject. But I was to realize quickly that his involvement with the Mary Rose went much deeper than just the scholarship of the bow. He was a trustee for many years, and a champion for the importance of the ship right to the end. Over my thirteen years steering the project of creating a new museum through hazardous shoal waters, often struggling to ensure the very survival of the project given the huge financial headaches, he was always at my side with support, encouragement, and when required, the ability to put his public persona forward to champion the cause. At one stage, when all looked lost, he initiated a two-page spread in a national daily paper which rallied support through sensational headlines and emotional words about the importance of one of our great national treasures. At key times in our campaign, he would unhesitatingly come down to offer his support by giving a talk or speaking to the media. His name was a huge draw; his words invariably apposite and stirring.

The personal joy was to get to know him as a friend, and he would stay with me and my wife, Jenny, when visiting Portsmouth. Dinners and long evenings chatting, perhaps with a tumbler of whisky in hand, were memorable. Conversations roamed everywhere, sparkling with intellectual debate and mischievous stories, always laced with delightful, clever humour. The twinkle in his eyes never dimmed. The first time he stayed, on arrival at breakfast and in answer to how he had slept, his reply was that it had been perfect until the tsunami hit us, which caused him to sit bolt upright in a panic. It was the first train of the day, and our house is alongside the railway line at Bosham. Thankfully, such a rude awakening did not preclude further stays.

We should visit him in Charlbury and latterly at Avington, and conversations continued where they had been left off. He remained deeply interested in the progress of the Mary Rose as we progressed towards the new museum. In 2007, he accompanied us on a boat to spend a day over the wreck site for the 25th anniversary of the raising of the ship. With Margaret Rule at his side, his stories poured forth, tying in with those of others who had been there on that momentous day. (Rough weather had delayed the lift and Tim missed the critical moment to resume filming somewhere.)

Another major visit was the day we showed both Tim and Margaret around the new museum before the official opening to the public. Margaret, by this stage, was in a wheelchair having been, in her words 'crippled by too many years on my knees, excavating'. They toured the museum with tears in their eyes. This was the fruition of their labours – as much as anyone's – some thirty-five years before, and their dreams had been fulfilled. It was so important to us that these two massively important figures pronounced their full approval of our interpretation of the ship and the artefacts.

For the official opening of the museum in 2013, both were there in prominent positions. Tim began the day at Southsea Castle, where King Henry had been in 1545, with the sight of the Mary Rose sinking less than a mile out to sea. He revelled in explaining the importance of the ship and the role of the archers to the world's press and discussed the weapons with the archers who had assembled there to shoot fire-arrows towards the wreck site. Yet again, his championship of the Mary Rose spread across the nation and far beyond.

Behind this famous face and voice lay a true gentleman of great charm, of deep scholarship and with an impressive strategic grasp of history. His unswerving, wonderful wit and exquisite manners remained with him throughout. From what Jenny and I got to see, he put others before himself, showing sensitivity and concern that, perhaps, would surprise many. I ended my last letter to him, one that he never received, by sending him our love and by telling him that the Mary Rose saluted him.'

***

Margaret Rule began her university life studying chemistry but changed direction, after working awhile at the Beecham Laboratories, to a course in archaeology. In the early sixties, Margaret was a member of the Chichester's archaeological committee. Along with Barry Cunliffe, she worked on test excavations in a Fishbourne field after some Roman remains had been found there. These preliminary examinations of the field soon revealed what we know as Fishbourne Palace – rooms and rooms of beautiful mosaics. When the museum was built in 1968, Margaret was appointed its curator, a post she held until 1969. At the behest of Alexander McKee, she agreed to assist him in his quest to discover the precise location of the grave of the Mary Rose. This, of course, occurred during her time at Fishbourne. Margaret learned to dive.

In 1971 the Mary Rose was finally located, and the site leased from the Crown at £1 per annum. (The site of the wreck had, in fact, been identified in 1836.) Then, the real work began resulting in the extraordinary feat of engineering, which saw a huge iron cage constructed under and around the wreck and lifted to the surface. Since 1545, the Mary Rose had lived in the muddy depths of the Solent: in 1982 she was recovered into daylight. The story is an amazing one and Margaret's book *The Mary Rose – The Excavation and Raising of Henry VIII's Flagship* is as exciting as any thriller.

Margaret's husband, Arthur, died in 2014 and the year before her own death. She had lived with Parkinson's Disease and crippling arthritis during her final years. Nick asked Tim to present the eulogy at his mother's funeral. Their close friendship made it a natural choice. On the occasion of my visit, we listened to a recording of the beautifully-crafted speech with moistening eyes. Tim spoke from the heart and, in his fondness for her, could not control the occasional gulp of emotion. Tim does not talk about Margaret: he addresses Margaret direct. Nick kindly permitted my use of this eulogy and I here transcribe it.

> 'Dearest Margaret! I speak to you, where your high, bright spirit lives, not to what you have left behind – to which we shall say farewell, in a few moments; sadly, because your physical presence was familiar, and so loved as the outward expression, the carapace, of what was so fair, so rich, so courageous, so indomitable within.
>
> Your son, Nick, has done me the honour of asking me to say a few words, just as you honoured me, Margaret, time and time again, by commissioning me and trusting me with the care of the Mary Rose bows, which I tried carefully to fulfil over many years. Fishbourne Palace seems a long-ago, magnificent achievement of yours, which I marvelled at, not knowing you then. But you left the land and plunged into

the murky waters and the silt of the Solent, to save HMS Mary Rose, to reveal once again the truth of history. And that is when I first knew you. Your desk in Portsmouth was filled with books, reports, research into all the disciplines you were busy mastering: late medieval shipbuilding, rigging, arming, military organization. Then one day in 1979, one diver discovered, in the silt, something which he thought was very important. He handed it to another top diver, who brought it on land. It was a nearly seven-foot stake. But the question was, to start with, looking at it – was it a pike staff? 'No' you said, 'that is our first longbow! Now wait, there is a book here somewhere – here it is.'

Tim expertly conjured a picture of the hopelessly over-burdened desk, and this dedicated woman anxious, as quickly as possible, to locate the book she knew to be there, and so get the best help possible, hands scrabbling about among the papers to find Tim's *Longbow – a social and military history*. He proceeded to add a monologue that further lifted the spirits of the congregation immediately.

"'Who is this man, Hardy? We must get him!" (It was a book I published in 1976. I had been part of a three-man team: Professor Peter Pratt, Professor of Crystal Physics of the Imperial College of Science and Technology, and John Levy, as far as I know, the only Professor of Wood Science

49

ever in this country, also of Imperial College, and already charged with the care of all the timber below surface and above, of the Mary Rose. And we – this little team – were experimenting in the capabilities and studying the history of the great medieval longbow.) When you called us in to aid, Margaret, we raced down, hair flying, to Portsmouth.'

Without any effort on its own part, Tim's few skilfully chosen words caused the congregation to see before its many eyes, two white-coated boffins led by an enthusiastic and 'let's-grasp-the-nettle' Robert Hardy, running, cartoon like, a few feet above the road from London to Portsmouth Dockyard. The pews creaked slightly as the mourners rearranged themselves in their respectful mirth. Tim continued.

'And so began the long thrilling task you put into our hands. You asked us to care for the restoration and exploration of one-hundred-and-thirty-eight complete bows, and research the broken pieces of many more, and told us that we could test the capabilities of up to three bows, even to destruction.

Brave and trusting Margaret! – a task which was only finished this year. You honoured us greatly, and my gratitude will never fade until we can carry on our evocation of the past; and practise our mental marksmanship at the butts of Elysium. So often we talked, laughed, ate, drank, shared our aspects of this particular task together, with your dear Arthur, whose death so profoundly wounded you and whom you hastened to join, where he can hear you and you can run together. At this last earthly moment, I know that your spirit will never leave us, and I send you my love, my admiration, my gratitude for giving me half – probably the better half – of my life's work. I am profoundly honoured, Ma'am.'

What a send-off! Nick is rightly proud of his mother and most thankful to Tim for this well-earned tribute.

Tim and Margaret

# The Battlefields Trust

Whenever Tim and I drove towards or past a famous or not-so-famous battle site, it would be pointed out to me with excitement and enthusiasm. I genuinely would be keen to know more. Once apprised, however, I knew I should be questioned closely next time we passed the same way. It is good to be able to pinpoint likely battlefields and so put a place to a name, making sense of all that one learnt from the classroom history books.

'What happened in that field?' Tim might wave an index finger in front of my eyes. There was always something of the schoolmaster about him, inherited, no doubt, from his father, though you'd probably get a snort of derision for suggesting it.

Once these sites are identified and absorbed into the memory, other things fall into place such as the geography of the place, the nearest town, lost villages lying in between. Questions arise. Long before blood was drawn in the field, were wealthy Romans and Britons luxuriating in the villas of the area? Did they plunge in the baths or bathe in the plunges located a little further down that road over there? More important, perhaps, what changed in England after that battle was done? O yes, battlefields are certainly worth getting to know, and they can be the key to so much more and, quite simply, a jolly good place to start. Howard Simmons, the Chairman of the Battlefields Trust here pays tribute to the President of the Battlefields Trust – Robert Hardy CBE FSA:

> 'When Robert Hardy sadly died in August 2017, there were many obituaries, which recalled and paid tribute to his outstanding career as an actor on stage, television and in films. Indeed, Robert became a much-loved celebrity and household name for his depictions of characters such as the Earl of Leicester in *Elizabeth R*, Winston Churchill in *The Wilderness Years* (he won a BAFTA and worldwide acclaim for this) and, yes, the vet, Farnon. However, a less reported dimension of Robert's life that was every bit as important to him was his contribution to historical, archaeological and battlefield studies.

He personally pioneered the serious academic study of the English longbow and its role in medieval warfare. He became internationally recognized for his writings and publications on this subject, particularly his two major studies *Longbow* and *The Great Warbow. From Hastings to the Mary Rose*. Robert became an enthusiastic member of the Battlefields Trust in 1993, its founding year, and subsequently became a Trustee and Board Member serving in this capacity until 2010 when he was appointed as the first Patron of the Trust. In 2011, following the death of the great military historian, Richard Holmes, he replaced him as President of the Trust.

The Battlefields Trust has benefited enormously from the support and encouragement that Robert Hardy generously provided to us over these many years, officiating at battlefield dedications and commemoration, and speaking at seminars and conferences. His special interests were in medieval battles and warfare, the role of the longbow, in particular. It was, therefore, a fitting tribute to his memory that the Battlefields Trust journal first published an article, which Robert prepared for the Trust, on the battle of Homildon Hill.

We wish to give proper recognition to Robert Hardy's commitment to and achievements in the area of battlefield interpretation and preservation. He served not only on important committees, such as the English Heritage Battlefields Panel and the boards of the Royal Armouries and, of course, the Mary Rose Trust alongside that of the Battlefields Trust. But it was as an active campaigner using his contacts and expertise to advance the cause of battlefields as key educational resources. One example of this was his work with the Naseby Battlefield Project, and students of Abbeyfield School in Northampton on the recording of 'The Sound of Battle' a downloadable audio-trail for visitors to the battlefield of Naseby, which won the 2010 'Heritage Award for Work with Children and Young People'.

Robert Hardy had a warm, engaging, and generous personality and was a wonderful Patron and President of the Battlefields Trust leaving a lasting legacy'.

When Tim became the President of the Trust, he, among many other things, created the 'President's Award' an annual prize to recognize an outstanding contribution to the work of the Trust. In the first year, it was presented to Martin Marix Evans, the military historian and author of over two dozen books on the two World Wars. As he lived in Northamptonshire it was natural that, at some point, he would turn his attention to the Battle of Naseby…

'I got to know Robert Hardy when I was invited to become a trustee of the Battlefields Trust. Robert had spoken at a conference organized by the Trust to examine the weapons and tactics of medieval warfare so that we could gain a better understanding of how a given field of battle might be visualized as the setting of conflict, describing the performance of the longbow in the hands of a skilled soldier. It was a riveting exposition.

Robert's contribution to the deliberations of the board of Trustees showed us that there was much more than a supremely talented actor come among us. The wisdom of his remarks steadied the more excitable of us. I recall clearly the gentle, restraining hand on my arm when one of our more over-enthusiastic members advocated an unrealistic course of action, and Hardy's intervention to make a proposition in quiet, reasoned tones, instead of the reaction I was so close to giving and in a way sure to offend rather than persuade.

In addition to the relatively light task of Trust business, I was much concerned with the development of the battlefield of Naseby to become a place well-furnished with explanatory notices, convenient parking places, and good viewpoint installations, so that visitors could guide themselves on a tour of the field of battle and develop their own interpretation of the fight of 1645. Broadcasts on television dealing with British history were becoming much more popular after the turn of the century, with much use being made of re-enactments by enthusiasts correctly clad and carrying appropriate weapons. However, we had no buildings in which we could offer such things, nor had we the large budgets required to create them.

If we could not show film of people dressed up and marching about some suitable place we pretended was Naseby in 1645 to give the eye-witness experience, what could we do? It came to us that we could offer instead an ear-witness opportunity. We could populate the landscape with the sound of battle and the voices of those who were there. I made tentative enquiry and Robert gave the idea his approval. But the cost of hiring actors and studios appeared to be prohibitive until we settled on a satisfactory scheme and devised a project with a local arts college – Abbeyfield School, Northampton.

At this point it became clear that we needed more help. To make a series of short dramatic episodes was relatively straightforward but it was also necessary to set each episode in the correct context as well as to preserve the policy of each episode relating to a specific viewpoint while preserving the freedom to allow the visitor to stop at the viewpoint in whatever order found convenient. The answer was to write introductory texts to be delivered in an alternative voice and style, and this Robert Hardy agreed to do for a token fee. In the event, he made sure that this charity benefitted from his token fee.

A collection of photocopied documents, the most recent from about 1690, was assembled to give the appropriate material for the students to begin their work. They drafted a lively script, expanding the simple story to include vivid personal accounts and designed to provide a sound track appropriate to each of the ten viewpoints on the visitors' circuit. The passages were then linked with the narrative text Robert had presented to set the scene for each.

On the day of recording, the students arrived with their teacher and Robert's driver delivered him to the studio door. To me Robert was the actor who had appeared in *Henry V, Elizabeth R* and *All Creatures Great and Small* but to the students he was the physical manifestation of his character – the Minister for Magic himself, Dr Cornelius Fudge!

The first thing was to get the connecting narrative read, with the students listening so that the contextual material was known to everyone. Robert used a small studio for this and we were able to watch him at work. That complete, we moved to the large studio to record the dramatic episodes, each of which had a cast of at least six male and female voices. Without prompting, one of the readers turned to Robert to seek confirmation that his delivery was satisfactory, and soon the mature actor and his novices were working together as colleagues.

In one of the sections, a young man, who had put aside his school jumper to remain cool in shirtsleeves, stumbled repeatedly over a particular phrase and was clearly somewhat ashamed and dismayed. Robert quickly suggested an approach to the problem: 'Perhaps it would help to change the rhythm a little and perhaps alter this word.' He offered a synonym as a possibility. They tried again, and the expression of pure delight on the young fellow's face as all went well was a joy to see. It was a lesson from a master that that chap will never forget! Of course, Robert certainly did not need to swathe himself about with airs and graces: children see through that sort of thing, anyway. I have no doubt that the lad was rewarded with a beaming smile from Robert as soon as he overcame the difficulty.'

# The Battle of Homildon Hill

The Battle of Homildon Hill 14th September, 1402 in Tim's most fascinating account may not be every reader's cup of tea. However, no one will fail to enjoy his masterly prose and the grasp of history displayed in his article. It really speaks for itself, and I am most grateful to the Battlefields Trust for permission to use it here along with the introductory article by the author, Clive Hallum-Baker. They first appeared in *Battlefield*, the magazine of the Battlefields Trust.

'In the summer of 2012, at the start of the build-up to the 500th anniversary of the battle of Flodden, the Remembering Flodden Project was honoured and delighted when Robert Hardy agreed to travel to the far north of England to speak about the archers at Flodden. This was to be more than just a fleeting visit as Robert was keen to see how the longbow had been used, not just on Flodden Field, but also on the battlefields of Halidon Hill, near Berwick-upon-Tweed, and Homildon Hill, near Wooler. The talk was an immediate sell-out, in fact, much more than a sell-out, and additional seating had to be installed in the beautifully decorated Lady Waterford Hall in Ford village, but even so there was a long list of people hoping for cancellation tickets.

The first day of his visit was spent around Flodden showing Robert the routes taken by the two opposing armies to the conflict, followed by a detailed tour of the battlefield itself. Lunchtime was an opportunity to listen to Robert as he recounted memories of his remarkable career on stage and screen, quoted from *Henry V* or slipped into the stentorian tones of a wartime Winston Churchill.

That evening, from the respectful hush when the great man arrived, the rapt attention of the audience during his talk, to the prolonged applause, the talk itself was a masterpiece.

Robert, of course, declined the use of a microphone. Testing the acoustics, 'Can you hear me at the back?' he asked, 'For I have more!' More was not needed; every word was clear distinct and heard throughout the hall.

The talk was, as expected, masterful, a combination of expert knowledge of the weapon, instinctive appreciation of tactics and an understanding of historical context. A few light touches of humour and the inimitable Hardy delivery made this an evening to remember. In a more relaxed mode, the next day was spent looking first at Halidon Hill, overlooking Berwick, followed by one of Robert's great interests, Homildon Hill near Wooler, some ten miles to the south of Flodden Field. Here we were met by Jim Short, the owner and farmer of Homildon Hill, and conveyed by Land Rover to all the strategic points of the battlefield.

The summit of Homildon Hill is not renowned for culinary delights, but, on this occasion, a lunch of local game pie and Doddington cheese, complemented by a rather fine claret, served in the lee of the vehicle, provided both sustenance and inspiration. The descent from the summit in the Land Rover was interesting, bordering on the terrifying. Once on the lower levels of the hill the topography and tactics of the battle seemed to merge and come into focus. Robert modified his earlier views of the conflict, and this was the inspiration for his reappraisal of the battle of Homildon Hill.'

I am pleased to include, from time to time, in this book, the chance to hear from Tim's very fountain pen, for from his pen we hear him speak so eloquently. Do you not become quickly aware of the labour of love that this essay was? Tim gives a little background to the battle, sufficient to enable the inquisitive reader to delve deeper if this period of history did not feature in his or her schooling.

## Homildon Hill by T.S.R. Hardy

**Homildon Hill (now called Humbleton Hill, near Wooler (National Grid reference NT 968294))** By the year 1402, only four years into a troubled reign, King Henry IV (Bolingbroke) was preoccupied by the revolt in Wales led by Owain Glyndwr. In Scotland the new men of influence, Robert, duke of Albany, and Archibald, earl of Douglas, felt the moment ripe for an invasion of England. An early incursion into English territory was defeated by the English at Nisbet on 22 June 1402, although some authorities place this encounter north of the Tweed near Duns while others prefer a location at Nisbet, just north of Wooler. However, a second invasion happened in August, when Douglas led 10,000 Scots into Northumberland, and as far south as Newcastle. The Scots, loaded with massive booty which slowed their movements, aimed to return home, heading for a crossing of the Tweed at Coldstream. They were intercepted by the earl of Northumberland who shadowed them closely, forcing them to face their army southwards, their backs towards Scotland. The Scots soon had to contend with another danger from the south. The king had ordered Northumberland's son, Henry Percy, the famous and impetuous 'Hotspur' to move north as fast as he could, for Wales where he was dealing with the Glyndwr revolt. Hotspur had been acting as mentor to young Henry, Prince of Wales, who was nominally the commander of the royal forces. Although only fourteen, Henry was showing remarkable skills as a soldier and tactician, which would one day lead to his victory at Agincourt, and to his being acknowledged as 'Heritier de France' (the heir of France).

The forces of Percy and Northumberland united, and together with the Scottish earl of March, George de Dunbar, blocked Douglas's northbound Scots at Milfield and forced them to take up a north-facing position of defence on the slopes of Homildon Hill. George de Dunbar had fallen out with Archibald Douglas over whose daughter would marry the heir to the Scottish throne and placed himself at the service of Henry IV.

There are two rough contemporary accounts of the battle, one Scottish, the 'Scotichronicon' of Walter Bower, and one English, Thomas Walsingham's 'Historia Anglicana' both of which in essence tell the same story. There is also a third account by John Hardying, who was present at the battle, but it tells us almost nothing about the detail of the action. What we learn from the accounts is that on 14 th September 1402, two, roughly equal, armies faced each other, the Scots on the lower slopes of Homildon Hill, the English on the flat, then slightly rising ground near the east-west road, which exists today in more modern form. Because the Scots had been forced to face north, the English were facing roughly south, looking straight up Homildon Hill.

That the Scottish position was on the lower slopes is unquestionable. Had they been higher, they would have been caught on ground that was so steep as to make manoeuvre impossible and they would have been unable to escape north or south due to the topography. The lower slopes seen today offer ridged and layered positions, caused probably by naturally tumbled ground from higher up the 1,000ft hill, and possibly trenched by the Scots that September. The Scots formed up in schiltrons or sheltrons, compact bodies of troops forming a battle array, shield wall or phalanx. The term is most often associated with Scottish pike formations during the Wars of

Scottish Independence in the late thirteenth and early fourteenth centuries. Ahead of the English right flank is a second substantial hill, called then, as now, Harehope Hill. It is on this hill that many have supposed the English archers were flung forward against the Scottish left, which must have bent back round the contour of Homildon, in order to refuse their flank. It is suggested that the archer force was thus detached from the main English Army, facing the Scots across a large defile. It is this point against which I argue that it would be madness to 'detach' an archer force, which could be cut off and routed, after the manner of the English debacle at Bannockburn in 1314. Archers with their wings unprotected were hopelessly vulnerable. Further, Professor John Childs (Emeritus Professor of Military History, Leeds University) has argued that the received translation of Walsingham's account, which gave rise to the Harehope theory, is wrong: the passage had been taken to mean: 'Our men climbed a hill opposite the Scots – i.e. another hill, Harehope – and 'Our archers were drawn up in a valley' – which could mean the valley between Harehope and Homildon, known as Monday Cleugh. But the original Latin – which reads: *Montem Scotis oppositum conscenderunt, nec mora nostril sagittarii, in valle constitute, sagittas miserunt ad Scotorum cuneum, et eos descensum quomodolibet provocarent* – is better translated 'Our men left the road on which they were assembled and climbed the hill opposite the Scots; without delay our archers who were drawn up in the vale, volleyed at the Scottish schiltron to provoke them into coming down.' The inference is that the Scots on Homildon were faced by the English, north of the hill, in the vale or valley which rises gently towards to hill's foot, and that the archers advanced to their front and shot massed volleys into the Scots above them. Douglas, galled by arrowshot, would hardly have charged down into the defile that separates Homildon from Harehope; Walsingham, properly read, indicates that Douglas charged down the hill straight towards the English archers deployed right across the front and wings of their army.

Scotichronicon says that the main English force was impatient to attack on Hotspur's orders, but the earl of March reined Hotspur back saying that, as at Falkirk in 1298, the archers could easily penetrate the Scottish ranks and defeat them. Walsingham reports 'the English archers shot without pause from where they were drawn up in the dale.' It is also quite clear, if you stand on Harehope, that the refused left flank of the Scots on Homildon is barely reachable by archery. Walsingham continues that the Scots shot their own volleys 'but they felt the weight of our arrows, which fell like a storm of rain, and so they fled.' This riposte had failed either from poor archery discipline, or lack of adequate numbers. The Scots were up against the best military archers in the world.

Let us follow Walsingham a little further: 'The earl of Douglas…saw the flight of his archers [probably round the south-east side of Homildon] so seized a lance and rode down the hill with a troop of his horse, trusting too much in his equipment and that of his men, who for three years had been improving their armour, and strove to rush on the archers.' Had he charged left-handed towards Harehope, he would have exposed his flank to Hotspur's barely restrained cavalry. Let us accept he charged straight down on the English archers in front of him. Walsingham goes on: 'When the archers saw this [the charge] they retreated, but still shooting so vigorously, so resolutely, so effectively that they pierced the armour, perforated the helmets, split the lances and pierced all the equipment with ease.' The earl of Douglas was pierced with five wounds, in spite of his elaborate armour. Douglas survived the battle with the loss of an eye and was taken into captivity by Percy. At Shrewsbury, in 1403, he fought alongside his former adversary Hotspur and again survived but this time, with the loss of a testicle.

The rest of the Scots Army fled, pursued at last by Hotspur's frustrated cavalry. Walsingham again: 'In this fight no lord or knight received a blow, but God Almighty gave the victory miraculously to the English [and Welsh] archers alone, and the magnates and men-at-arms remained idle spectators of the battle.' In what direction did the Scots flee? 'Towards the river Tweed' where it is said 500 drowned. My belief is that they ran to their left, into the Harehope valley and across that hill and down to the flatter 'Red Riggs' so called for the slaughter that occurred there. They ran towards the north, towards home, and largely failed to get round the English right. Had the English archers been on Harehope, the Scots could not have streamed across it at its cleugh or cleuch.

To walk the hills, and to think medievally, the battle becomes clear. At this stage, as an 'envoi' it is worth quoting from Oman's great 'Art of War in the Middles Ages':

'At Homildon Hill the English bowmen had won one more of their typical victories over the Scots – a victory entirely of the type of Dupplin or Halidon. A Scottish army, trying to make its way home after a raid into Northumberland, had been intercepted and forced to endeavour to cut its way through. Formed in the usual heavy columns…they had taken their position high on the hillside, where they found the English archer circling round and at the same time moving up against their front. When Douglas charged, and his masses rolled down the slope, the archery gave back, more slowly on the wings, more rapidly in the centre, so that the advancing column found itself in a semi-circle of converging arrow-shot…so deadly had been the arrow shower that the Scots had never been able to close.'

The phrase 'the archers circling round' suggests the usual positioning of strong bodies of them on both wings, which would include a right-wing reach embracing the refused Scottish left, but still vitally and firmly a part of the English army; it is this that gives rise to the theory of a detached force of them on Harehope. TSRH

*  *  *

Following a lunch trip somewhere, I remember this conversation when Tim drove home afterwards:

'Have coffee, won't you?'

'Thanks, though I shall have to get away sharpish this afternoon.'

'Good, I have some work to do,' he said with a grin. 'I am putting the finishing touches on an incident upon Homildon Hill.'

'Some sort of battle?'

'Some sort, yes.'

'Good day for your archers, was it?'

'Yes, and the earl of Douglas was left with five holes to prove it!'

'Was that the place you visited a week or so ago? You thought it cold, I remember.'

Tim gave a snort. 'Bloody cold.'

I pursued it no further as I might have had to concede no knowledge whatsoever of Homildon Hill! But what meticulous enthusiasm Tim displays in this essay. He manages to convey the excitement of the battle even as he charts the battle in sober military terms. It is quite a gem and reveals yet another facet of this extraordinary man.

# Towards Agincourt

Tim was fond of Anne Curry (Now Dean of Humanities and Professor of Medieval History at Southampton University) and was always singing her praises in admiration of her work. Anne writes warmly of their friendship. She describes herself as 'medieval historian with special interests in the Hundred Years War and, more specially, Agincourt.' Anne was the adviser to the Royal Armouries exhibition at the Tower of London and, inter alia, Chairman of the Trustees of 'Agincourt 600' set up to commemorate the anniversary, and instrumental in achieving a proper monument for the battlefield. She is a prolific author.

'I cannot remember when I first met Tim, or when we first communicated about our mutual interest in the battle of Agincourt. Of course, I knew him from his splendid portrayal of Robert Dudley, Earl of Leicester in *Elizabeth R*. For me he was Dudley – all charm, bravado, and intelligence. I was less interested in vets in North Yorkshire, though, as my grandparents lived close to where the actual practice had been, *All Creatures Great and Small* did not altogether elude my television viewing. Possessing a copy of Tim's *The Longbow* (1976 followed by countless editions) made me well aware that there was another string to his bow.'

This interjection may be apposite. Of course, we know the origin of that expression and that it would be foolhardy to travel anywhere as a bowman without 'another string'. This and the sheer strength required to string a longbow, let alone to draw a longbow, was brought home to me when Tim told me of the time during an after-dinner speech, he prevailed upon two Royal Marines guarding the mess to attempt to string the bow he had brought with him. Sadly, they failed. I was rather hoping that this had occurred at the dinner on board HMS Victory to which Tim had been invited by Vice Admiral Sir Charles Montgomery (one time Second Sea Lord and C-in-C Naval Home Command and Flag ADC to the Queen, among other posts). Alas, that was not the case and I have been unable to track down where it occurred. However, at this juncture, a word from Sir Charles might fit in here quite well after all.

'I met Robert on a few occasions, happily always at relatively small, intimate social occasions. Each was a great pleasure for me. Indeed, the greatest tribute I can offer is that as I bade farewell to him on each occasion, it felt as though I was parting with a long-standing friend. He quietly oozed warmth, humour, interest. Despite his obvious professional success, I recall Robert as touchingly modest, even self-deprecating, never seemingly taking himself too seriously. I remember the ready twinkle on that eye and that voice…rich in tone and resonant, no doubt honed and re-honed during his stage career. He loved conversation and was quite simply very good at it; partly because he was well read and informed but also because he was a good listener. He was good to listen to as well. And especially so when he talked about the longbow. He made this singular subject his own, never tiring of talking about it and answering countless questions on the subject – questions he must have fielded many times before but always skilfully leaving the impression that the last question just might have never been asked before. If he were to walk through the door as I write,

I feel sure we would pick up as we had left off, without any awkwardness born of absence.'

All that was so true and so many shared this experience. And on that note, we return to Anne's recollections and continue our journey toward Agincourt.

'The first meeting in the flesh and the first real appreciation of his expertise in the history of archery came, I think, with a weekend conference at Rewley House, Oxford University's Department of Continuing Education (now, better known as Kellogg College), I organized jointly with Michael Hughes, the County Archaeologist of Hampshire in November 1991. Tim was part of a distinguished line-up of speakers on Arms and Armies in the Hundred Years War, and his sparkle as well as his erudition was clear from the start. It fell to me to liaise with the speakers in order to produce a volume from the conference (Boydell Press 1994). Chapter 10: Robert Hardy – *The Longbow*, which begins in Tim's characteristically pithy manner: 'My subject is the longbow, the weapon itself.' His qualifications for this chapter were impeccable, Trustee of the Royal Armouries, Trustee of and Consultant to the Mary Rose Trust, member of the then recently established Battlefields Panel of English Heritage – I much regret he and I overlapped only by one meeting when I was invited to join this panel many years later – as well as a longbow archer of many years' experience.

Working with Tim on the chapter was a delight, not least because of his keenness to debate Agincourt: for his article he had prepared a splendid set of maps suggesting how the troops had been drawn up at the battle (and he slipped in another for Crécy!). The 'phone line was often buzzing, as it most certainly was after our next encounter in the field, at a one-day event in Norwich Cathedral in October 1996 organised by the Norfolk Heraldry Society in honour of Sir Thomas Erpingham.'

At this point we might join Matthew Strickland, professor of Medieval History at Glasgow University and collaborator with Tim (i.e. joint author) in *The Great Warbow - from Hastings to the Mary Rose* (Sutton Publishing 2005). Matthew takes on the telling of the tale:

'Most occasions spent with Tim were memorable, but one in particular stands out and captures something of his remarkable character and the charisma that made him such a well-loved public figure. In 1996, a one-day conference was held in Norwich Cathedral to celebrate Sir Thomas Erpingham, the famous commander of the archers at the battle of Agincourt, who is buried in the cathedral, and who has given his name to the finely carved archway that leads into the cathedral close. Erpingham was a character dear to Tim, who with wry humour commissioned a portrait of himself as 'old Sir Thomas' at the moment in Shakespeare's *Henry V* when the king, wishing to remain incognito as he toured the English camp on the eve of Agincourt, asks Erpingham to lend him his cloak (Act iv Scene i). It was a chilly and misty October morning as Tim, sharply dressed in his favourite countryman's green tweed three-piece suit, met with me, with Anne Curry, Matthew Bennett, other speakers, and the conference organisers in the cathedral a little ahead of the start of the proceedings, to review the running order of the lectures and to check the equipment. A very large projector screen had been set up at the east end of the nave. Tim, who was scheduled to speak mid-way through the morning session, almost always lectured without notes, and preferred to talk impromptu with a series of slides. This was a natural choice for such an accomplished actor, and it gave his talks a memorable zest and spontaneity. As a very sizeable audience gathered, filling the nave, Tim handed the technician a carousel full of slides – this was just before the age of 'Powerpoint' and easy access to a host of digital images on the web – which were to serve as his visual props for a lecture on the role of the archers at Agincourt. They included some wonderful pictures of longbows raised from the Mary Rose, and of their conservation and testing, in which he had played so important a role. The conference began well enough, but only a few minutes before it was Tim's turn to speak, the gloomy morning suddenly gave way to bright autumnal sunshine. Light flooded through the great west window of the cathedral, down the nave and on to the projector screen, making it quite impossible to see any of the images projected on to it. What was to be done? Without slides and no notes, Tim's talk seemed doomed, and now a restless audience, many of whom no doubt had come specifically to hear him talk, looked set to be disappointed.

As we conferred in awkward consternation, Tim suddenly proclaimed, 'I'll give them the Harfleur and the Agincourt speeches!' And, stepping forward, he began that most famous of Shakespeare's speeches: "Once more unto the breach…" and then, "This day is called the Feast of Crispian…" Within seconds, the audience was rapt. Tim's distinctive voice rang through the cathedral as he declaimed the part he knew so well. He had played the role of Henry V in the 1960 BBC adaptation of *Henry V* and the study of King Henry V, the battle of Agincourt and the longbow were a lifelong passion. But this was a bravura performance, made all the more thrilling by its spontaneity. As he strode up and down the nave, gesturing and stopping to address sections of the audience, during the Harfleur speech, as if they were part of the army, with his cadence remarkably textured and subtle, we were transported. "Be copy now to men of grosser blood, and teach them how to war." Then, in the Agincourt speech, as if for a moment, we were in the English host on the field of Agincourt and in the presence of Henry V himself. It was an extraordinary and quite magical few moments, with an almost tangible emotional charge filling the great medieval building. Then a short but deep silence, followed by wild applause. Tim had turned near disaster into a triumph, and quite stolen the show. It was an unforgettable experience, and one that his fellow speakers still recall with wonder and delight.'

Anne Curry continues:

'Once again, I found myself charged with editing a collection of papers from the day ('Agincourt 1415. Henry V, Sir Thomas Erpingham and the triumph of the English archers. Tempus Publishing 2000). This time, Tim was exceptionally busy in his acting – this was the Churchillian period I seem to remember. But he was happy to contribute a Foreword and kind enough to provide a photograph of a splendid portrait by Howard Morgan of himself as Sir Thomas. I know that playing the part of St Thomas

Erpingham gave him a particular thrill given the knight's role in command of the archers.

Around the time the book was published I had produced my 'The Battle of Agincourt. Sources and Interpretations' (Boydell Press 2000), about which Tim was particularly flattering. When promoted to a chair in the following year, the administration staff of the department of History at Reading used to love him to call asking to speak to 'Professor Anne'. He and I shared our hopes for the new Centre Historique médiévale at Azincourt and had them fully realized in the splendid building, which was completed in 2001, its entrance hall taking the form of a bow at full stretch, arrow and all. Tim's support for the initiative, and his fame in France where he was then playing Churchill in French ('De Gaullè celui qui a dit NON'), led to his wholly appropriate and much-loved involvement in the opening ceremony. At Azincourt Tim remains a much-appreciated true friend, playing a key role too in his opposition to the possible placing of a wind farm close to the battle site. At the opening I also recall his kindness to my children and those of Matthew Bennett, sharing with them in the weapons gallery his enthusiasm and knowledge in the way that only he could. Thus, are lifelong memories made.

When I produced my 'Agincourt, A New History' in 2005 (Tempus Publishing), Tim did not know what to think. 'What do you mean, the English may not have been as much outnumbered as previously thought?' But he was impressed by what he called my 'telephone directory' of soldiers on the campaign and all our discussions were fun. By this time he was heavily involved in the last stages of *The Great Warbow* with Matthew Strickland. If I produced a telephone directory, the Hardy and Strickland produced the bible. Both authors should be justifiably proud of their achievement. It is hard to imagine such a brilliant combination of experts in their different ways. *The Great Warbow* will remain the 'go-to' book for years to come.

Before too long things started heating up on another battle – Bosworth – where Leicestershire County Council were awarded a Heritage Lottery Fund to find the Bosworth battlefield. Tim was involved here as he had been in Azincourt, boosted by his presidency of the Battlefield Trust, which was commissioned to carry out the work. He was thrilled when Glenn Foard and his team made significant finds in the last months of the project. Tim supported me, as the historian on the project, and Glenn with advice and support throughout. What a line-up at the official launch of the findings in the splendid Leicestershire

County Hall in February 2010: not only Richard Holmes (the military historian who died the following year) but also the great Robert Hardy. And to see Tim in his characteristic 'astride' pose gazing at the new battlefield is etched on my memory. As for my husband, he could scarcely concentrate on driving with Tim's waxing lyrical on the back seat!

After the excitement of Bosworth, the promise of the 600th anniversary of Agincourt in 2015 dangled before us. Tim, again, was the natural choice for the working party, which began to meet at the Tower of London in 2012, not only for his expertise on the battle and its archers but also by dint of his being a past master of the Worshipful Company of Bowyers. Even when he felt unable to come in person, he maintained a strong interest and support, and we were thrilled that he was able to participate in the service of commemoration at Westminster Abbey on 29th October 2015, 600 years to the day that the news of Henry V's victory reached London.

Tim chose the passage he should read: the prologue to Act iv of Shakespeare's *Henry V*. He transported us to that moment when 'creeping murmur and the poring dark fills the wide vessel of the universe'. We heard the hum of either army, the secret whispers of each other's watch. The horses neighed; the armourers wielded their busy hammers. The

English sat patiently waiting the morrow. The royal captain walked from tent to tent visiting his host, giving his liberal eye to everyone, thawing cold fear. There was indeed ' a little touch of Harry in the night' thanks to the little touch of Tim —' actor and longbow expert' as he was billed in the order of service. He will indeed be remembered. No one who ever met him could forget him or cease to be thankful for knowing him.'

When one watches a recording of this service in Westminster Abbey - Tim's final Shakespeare performance - one cannot but be impressed by his immediate command of both words and congregation as Anne has observed above. Ninety on the very day, Tim acknowledged the Altar, the bishop and Their Royal Highnesses, the Duke of Kent and Princess Michael, before taking his position behind his personal lectern, a few paces from his seat at the north-east corner of the choir. He was assiduous in connecting with his audience by constant glances over his reading glasses. Sometimes they were enquiring glances as if to ensure the audience was keeping up with what Chorus was declaiming. Tim introduced the speech:

'Shakespeare speaks of the night of the 24th and 25th of October 1415, the night before Agincourt…

"Now entertain conjecture of a time

When creeping murmur and the poring dark

Fills the wide vessel of the universe.

From camp to camp through the foul womb of night

The hum of either army stilly sounds,

That fix'd sentinels almost receive

The secret whispers of each other's watch;

Fire answers fire, and through their paly flames

Each battle sees the other's umber'd face;

Steed threatens steed, in high and boastful neighs

Piercing the night's dull ear; and from the tents

The armourers, accomplishing the knights,

With busy hammers closing rivets up;

Give dreadful note of preparation:

The country cocks do crow, the clocks do toll,

And the third hour of drowsy morning name.

Proud of their numbers and secure in soul,

The confident and over-lusty French

Do the low-rated English play at dice;

And chide the cripple tardy-gaited night

Who, like a foul and ugly witch, doth limp

So tediously away. The poor condemned English,

Like sacrifices, by their watchful fires

Sit patiently and inly ruminate

The morning's danger, and their gesture sad

Investing lank-lean cheeks and war-worn coats

Presenteth them unto the gazing moon

So many horrid ghosts. O now, who will behold

The royal captain of this ruin'd band

Walking from watch to watch, from tent to tent,

Let him cry "Praise and glory on his head!"

For forth he goes and visits all his host,

Bids them good morrow with a modest smile

And calls them brothers, friends and countrymen.

Upon his royal face there is no note

How dread an army hath enrounded him;

Nor doth he dedicate one jot of colour

Unto the weary and all-watched night,

But freshly looks and over-bears attaint

With cheerful semblance and sweet majesty;

That every wretch, pining and pale before,

Beholding him, plucks comfort from his looks:

A largess universal like the sun,

His liberal eye doth give to every one,

Thawing cold fear, that mean and gentle all

Behold, as may unworthiness define,

A little touch of Harry in the night…'"

In grave sadness, Tim delivered 'so many horrid ghosts' and delicately drew out the word 'thawing' so subtly, so effectively in the phrase 'thawing cold fear'. The audience was just where Shakespeare intended. Tim concluded the excerpt with a priceless touch of genius in his pregnant pause after the name 'Harry' in the final phrase ' a little touch of Harry…in the night'.

Dr Sinclair-Rogers had many a contact with Tim as Bowyers' representative on the Royal Armouries' Agincourt Committee in 2007 and in the many roles he subsequently took on in connection with Agincourt 600. He too recalls the day of the Westminster Abbey service.

'Those of us on the Agincourt 600 Committee enjoyed his early contributions to our planning. One of his most emphatic preferences concerned the English pronunciation of Agincourt – the final 't' was fully sounded, but Azincourt, the village in France, was pronounced in the French manner and with a silent 't'. We dutifully followed this throughout our planning of the commemoration. One of his last performances in public was at the service to commemorate the 600th anniversary of the battle. This date was the actual anniversary and the day of Robert Hardy's 90th birthday! On the day of the service, I picked him up from his hotel – the Churchill, of course – early in the morning so that he could rehearse in the Abbey. My two granddaughters accompanied me as they were taking part in the service. Robert was delightful with the girls and made them feel very important. At the Abbey I was anxious that he had a copy of the text he was to read, so I offered him one I had brought along with me. 'Do not worry, dear boy' he said, 'I have a spare in this pocket, another in this pocket and a third in my overcoat.' Immediately he started to speak there was a great susurration around the Abbey at the sound of his distinctive voice. He is greatly missed.'

We might conclude these reminiscences of the Agincourt celebration by returning to Matthew Strickland and by permitting him to complete the picture and have the last word.

'There is a postscript with a pleasing symmetry. In 2015, Tim was present at the great ceremony in Westminster Abbey to commemorate the six hundredth anniversary of the battle of Agincourt. A veteran now more akin to Sir Thomas Erpingham but still as sharp and fiery as ever, he gave a reading from Shakespeare's 'Henry V', this time the Prologue from Act iv with its vivid portrait of the English army on the eve of the battle. Then, seated in the choir he watched in evident delight as a young actor from the RSC, Sam Marks, appeared in full armour as Henry V from behind the high Altar screen to deliver the great Agincourt speech. I suspect that Tim may have proffered advice from his own long experience, but to those of us present who had been in Norwich cathedral back in 1996, this new performance brought to mind memories of Tim's own speech and seemed a fitting symbol of the passing on of traditions, both in acting and of history, that Tim held so dear.'

***

Elsewhere, I mention Tim's sensitivity to atmospheres and memories that could be conjured so easily in ancient places. Neil recalls the first time he was taken to the battlefield of Agincourt.

'We arrived just before dusk after a day at Crécy. The plan had been to spend the following day at Agincourt, but Tim was anxious that I should see it as soon as possible. Tim had a unique way of firing up one's imagination of a medieval battle and I have marched around many a battlefield with him since. We walked into the muddy, ploughed field and, as we approached from the side of the woods where there had been erected a large Crucifix, the evening mist seemed to swirl from the woods and across the surface of the field. I was suddenly hit with a sense of foreboding and my ears were filled with the sounds of horses, clashing metal and the cries and shouts of many men. There was no one there at all. But Tim immediately suggested we return to the car (perhaps on account of the expression on my face) admitting later that he too had been most conscious of something other-worldly. Were the two of them treated to a momentary understanding of the horror of the heat of battle? Who knows?'

# Tim the Actor

## Memories from the acting world

Tim and Judi in Henry V

### Judi Dench CH DBE FRSA

Judi is well known as 'M', a part Tim coveted in later years. Her film work is impressive, and it is difficult to cite just a few gems as there are so many. Her early television appearances included work with Tim in *The Age of Kings* and, later, her voice was heard in *Middlemarch*, that rather splendid serialisation of

George Eliot's novel. Later, Judy gave memorable performances in *Cranford* and *Return to Cranford*. Of course, I cannot fail to mention the long-running *As Time Goes By* with the ever-patient Geoffrey Palmer. Judi has never spent a long time out of the theatre and 'off the boards'. I remember very well her Vulumnia in *Coriolanus* at Chichester Festival Theatre. She is a patron of 'Dragon Drama' the theatrical school for the young, as was Tim until his death. Dame Judi writes:

> 'While I was playing Princess Katherine in *Henry V* at the Old Vic with Donald Houston, I was also recording the same part in another version for television, in 1960, with Robert Hardy (known to his friends, always, as Tim). Different costumes, slightly different script, and slightly different performances, one for the stage and one for television. It seemed to me that Tim was the epitome of Henry V. In fact, there was absolutely nothing that he did not know about Henry V. He seemed to understand everything about him and, of course, was famously one of the few people in England who could draw a longbow. Oh, how we laughed! He had a wicked sense of humour! It was all a very long time ago, but I remember those glorious days and how much I learned from him – not only about Henry V, but about acting generally. I would do it all again and would not change a thing.

Not so long ago, I made a programme about trees, for the BBC. Tony Kirkham, who is head of the Arboretum at Kew, was part of the programme. Knowing that I was in the habit of planting trees for family and friends, he came to visit one day and brought me a yew tree to plant. This one could be traced back to a yew at Runnymede, so it seemed most appropriate to put Tim's name on it, as he had only just died, and it has become a perfect memorial to him, and a constant reminder of this remarkable man.'

Tim and Eileen as Hamlet and Ophelia

# Eileen Atkins DBE

Well known as a screenwriter and actress, Eileen had a good grounding in Shakespeare but, curiously perhaps, appeared only once with Tim long ago in Chicago. Eileen devised with Jean Marsh the popular television series, *Upstairs, Downstairs* and *The House of Elliot.* She has appeared, in recent years, in *Poirot, The Crown* and, of course, *Doc Martin.* But I believe she has been at her busiest on the stage. Dame Eileen tells me:

> 'I'm very happy that you are producing a book about Robert but sad that I only did *Hamlet* with him so many years ago. In that season in Chicago, he played both Hamlet and Henry V, and was brilliant in both. He was an immensely courteous actor and was both helpful and patient with me, his very young, Ophelia. His work in *An Age of Kings* was absolutely wonderful; he added a touch of glamour to the series. Good luck.

Tim as Alec in *Troubleshooters*

# Robert Lindsay

Although generally well known in film and on television, Robert is perhaps best known for *Citizen Smith*, and the witty *My Family*, with Zoe Wanamaker. On stage, he is a familiar face both in the West End and on Broadway, but he has a fond memory of his early work with Tim at the BBC. Robert Lindsay remembers:

> 'Robert was a real inspiration for me. *Twelfth Night* was my first television Shakespeare and Robert was such a support and encouraged me to express myself in the role of Fabian, which led to my being cast in six more of the Shakespeare plays for the BBC. *Twelfth Night* had such an incredible cast and, at first, I felt quite intimidated, but Robert took me under his wing, and I remember that production with much affection. We all had such fun! – and what more could you want from a Shakespeare play? Good fortune with the project.'

## Julian Fellowes – The Lord Fellowes of West Stafford

This versatile man sits in the Lords, acts, directs, and is a screenwriter and novelist. We remember him with Richard Briers in *Monarch of the Glen* in the character of Kilwillie. We have seen him in the Sharpe series and in the Bond film, *Tomorrow Never Dies*. He wrote *Gosford Park* and the popular series *Downton Abbey*. (Interestingly, Tim was eager for a part in *Downton Abbey*. Once – I was on the telephone to him – he mistook me for the young Fellowes as he must have been in a balloon of wishful thinking. Tim had just finished watching the latest episode a few minutes before my call and so the matter was on his mind. Sadly, I was unable to oblige.) Julian Fellowes recalls:

> 'Tim Hardy was an exceptional man, witty, funny (not always the same thing), clever, learned, and of course a wonderful actor. Above all, he was brilliant company. We were not so much great friends as friendly acquaintances, a relationship that some people, particularly Americans, often do not fully understand. To my mind, acquaintanceship is friendship without the burden of responsibility. No one telephones an acquaintance for help with a midnight flood! A friendly acquaintance is simply there to make the most of pleasant moments when chance brings you together. So it was with Tim. We would chat about how terrible the modern world was when we ran into each other in restaurants or at parties. That said, he did once pay me the greatest compliment I have ever received when he praised my first novel, *Snobs*, which he had just finished reading. 'When my mother was old,' he said, when we were together at some gathering, 'she always read the same book. At last,

I asked her why she didn't try a different volume. "Why should I?" she replied, "I can never remember the plot, but I know I enjoy it." And I am going to do the same with *Snobs*.' I cannot think of any praise in my whole career that has pleased me more. I shall miss him.'

Tim as Malcolm Campbell in *Speedking*

## Douglas Hodge

Douglas is an actor and director, known on stage on the large screen and the small. He is remembered as a member of Rumpole's notorious client family, the Timsons in Rumpole of the Bailey. He was a regular member of the cast in *Capital City*, he appeared in *Spooks* (as did Tim, but in another episode), and *Mansfield Park*. He gave a memorable performance in *Decline and Fall* more recently, as Evelyn Waugh's extravagantly seedy and complex character, Grimes. Much earlier, in *Middlemarch*, as Dr Tertius Lydgate, he was genuinely honoured to be cast alongside Tim. Douglas still holds to the awe and respect he felt for Tim. Here, he writes during stage rehearsals in New York:

'When I first worked with Robert, I realized I didn't actually know him, I just felt I did. Our first encounter was on the set of *Middlemarch* but he'd loomed large in my imagination before that because of the work I had watched him perform. One of the other actors I had obsessed over, in my twenties, was Richard Burton and, of course, Richard and Robert had been great friends since their university days. At last, in *Middlemarch* I finally got to work with someone whom I believed to be a true Shakespearean in the real sense of the tradition of my craft. There is such a lot about being a stage actor that is to do with learning and inheriting, with choices, inflections and, even, tricks of the trade. It is an inheritance if it is the building of an edifice of interpretation across time. Robert had an innate understanding of the streams and rivers of and in Shakespeare's language, and it ran through all his work.

It was serendipitous to meet him finally whilst plying our trade on television. From the first day of the first 'table read' I watched him like a hawk. His insouciance, his inner energy and, indeed, his audacity were all trademarks hard to resist. He, like others I had observed – Michael Gambon and Anthony Hopkins - had this magpie tendency to learn and collect.

The single greatest trick I learnt from him and something I have put into my own 'larder' was the way he used his text, however archaic or arcane, to capture whatever character it was with simple adjustments to the voice – the dropping of aitches, the leaving of words unfinished, the slowing of the voice the speeding up of the voice, the richness, the sourness, while still keeping to the character's class and position and rendering real, flawed, unpleasant or likeable. I strive to assimilate that ease of delivery.

He was an electric companion, a real storyteller, and an avid listener, who always held his own ground. He was one of a noble line of great British actors whose influence still pervades the work we are all doing.'

Tim in the BBC's first *David Copperfield*

# Nigel Havers – The Hon. Nigel Havers

Nigel is, of course, a familiar sight on stage and screen. He has turned his talent to most genres. He has appeared in *Downton Abbey, Midsomer Murders, Murder in Mind, Coronation Street, The Charmer, Don't Wait Up, A Horseman Riding By,* and countless other plays, shows and films. He has made memorable stage appearances in *Rebecca* and *Art* – I remember both very well. His versatility has cast him in many, many pantomimes. Perhaps his role as Randolph Churchill in *The Wilderness Years* is, for our purposes, the most significant. Nigel recalls an amusing incident for the Churchill chapter (q.v.) which is, quite simply: 'A brief snapshot of someone with the biggest heart and an exuberant love of life. He is sadly missed.'

Tim with James Murray

# James Murray and Sarah Parish

This wonderful husband-and-wife acting team suffered the loss of their first child, the result of a congenital heart defect. To help relieve their sorrow, they have, with the help of others, raised £5m for a new Paediatric Emergency and Trauma department at the University Hospital, Southampton. It is a magnificent effort. Sarah is known for her roles in *Merlin* and *Atlantis* and as that rather unpleasant, sinister, and not very upright Superintendent Bancroft, a part she brings to life most skilfully. James is known for *Primaeval*, in which he encountered all those extraordinary and ingeniously created prehistoric beasts, and a host of other roles. *Midsomer Murders, New Tricks, Chaos* and *McDonald and Dodds* are performances that spring to mind.

Towards the end of Tim's life, Sarah and James presented An Evening with Robert Hardy at the Theatre Royal, Winchester, and James made a poignant 'short' of Tim entitled *In Familia* with Nina Sosanya. This was Tim's final performance. James (Jim) brings to mind his first encounters with Tim:

'Growing up in Hereford, I was privileged enough to be surrounded by ancient British countryside, In fact, not far from where we lived stood a 1500-year-old yew tree that dominated a 15th century chapel. I know its age only because there was a plaque of certification endorsed by one,

Robert Hardy. The curious teenager in me questioned just who was this magician who could age such a magnificent tree with such confidence and accuracy? 'The funny bloke from *All Creatures*' came the answer from my parents. Thirty-five years later I discovered he was so much more than that.

I had acted in a Miss Marple episode with Robert about fifteen years ago and since then knew exactly how established and respected an actor he was. But it wasn't until 2014 that I got to know properly the great man. He had just moved to a village next to mine and it wasn't long before we were thrown together in a gig for 'Help for Heroes' [the UK Military Veterans Charity] where (along with Sarah) we narrated an abridged version of Kipling's life before a live audience. Waiting in the wings Robert (or, Tim, as he insisted I call him) regaled acting yarns of old to me; boozy adventures with Richard Burton, mischievous exchanges on stage with Judi Dench… I knew I was going to like this man and was completely swept up by his infectious and magnetic charisma.

And so blossomed a kind of teacher-pupil friendship whereby I should go to Tim's and sit and listen to him for hours on end. He would wax lyrical about all he was passionate about, and rail acerbically about all that made him baulk. Never a more refreshingly brutally honest man had I met – and one with such charm and intelligence to boot! In the few years I got to know Tim, I felt truly honoured to have been invited into his world and allowed to wander around the corridors of his superlative mind. He was a special person, and, above all, I count myself blessed to be able to call him my friend.'

## Nina Sosanya

Nina brings a special grace to her acting and has been seen on stage and television and in film – from *Anthony and Cleopatra* at the National Theatre to television's *Jonathan Creek, Silent Witness, Lewis* and *Dr. Who*. She has appeared at Stratford in *As you Like it* and *Love's Labours Lost*. Nina was Kate McKenzie in BBC's *Last Tango in Halifax* and Detective Chief Inspector Laura Porter in ITV's *Marcella*. She plays Leigh Henry in *Screw*. In the short film *In Familia*, made not long before Tim's death, written and directed by James Murray as a special tribute to Tim, Nina and Tim ad lib beautifully and convincingly within the framework given them by James. It is delightful, funny, and poignant all at the same time. Nina is perfect and Tim shows no loss of skill in this, his final appearance before the camera. Nina provides us with a final touching memory:

'Hello, Julien! Robert Hardy has been an acting hero of mine for a very long time. I've watched him all my life, bursting out of the television, crackling with energy and speed of thought. I've listened to him on the radio, and on audio books brilliantly narrating the Patrick O'Brien novels, and I have read his books. The experience of working with him was actually just as I'd imagined it might be - disciplined, fun, and with a healthy dose of anecdotes.

He improvised seamlessly, completely relaxed, sharp and witty – it was a joy to watch. It was also a joy to make him laugh, which I did a few times, and felt as though I had won an award! There aren't many people who glinted like Robert Hardy. To sit next to him, to share a whisky ('Good girl!'), to talk about theatre and history and the countryside; to act in a scene with him and try to work out how he does it (I don't know) were all such wonderful things. Robert was infinitely interesting and interested in everything. It was an absolute privilege to meet and to work with him.'

Tim during the filming of *In Familia,* his final role.

# Churchill

Few people need to be reminded of how readily Tim became identified with the person of Sir Winston. As a consequence, and his diligent research into the man, Tim's close association with the Churchill family developed. Oddly, Tim did not, at first, fancy playing the great man. 'N-no, I'm not even built like Churchill. No, I am not your man!' he declared to his agent. He even took the trouble to list those actors he thought better equipped to play the part. Interestingly, at the top of Tim's list of about ten names, was the much-admired Welsh actor, Anthony Hopkins.

Happily, Tim was prevailed upon, and the resulting television masterpiece, the series, *The Wilderness Years* gives us something rather special and as fresh today in its remastered DVDs as it was in the 1980s. And it was the start of Tim's long love affair with the character and person of Churchill. He would play the man on many occasions both on television and on stage – once in France, in French.

*The Wilderness Years* gave us Churchill all at sea and rejected in 1929 and in the political wilderness for the best part of a decade. Only very gradually was he restored during those years, bit by bit. This process is beautifully and accurately shown as slowly, very slowly his own party began to see the force of what he was saying. What a pity a fresh series giving us the wartime Churchill did not immediately follow. (But he returned to *All Creatures Great and Small* and, as Peter Davison tells us, decidedly more Churchillian than he had been in the earlier series.)

*The Wilderness Years* was certainly 'star-studded', the acting and direction perfect. During a Christmas break in the filming, Tim, still in the early stages of his capturing Churchill, was most anxious not to lose the voice, the timbre, and the character of both, and spent a difficult time with his family. On his return to the studios and after a morning's session, the director took him aside and asked, 'Where's Churchill gone?' Once recovered, he never lost it again.

As one might imagine, Tim's research was thorough, and the dress, the attitude, the inflexions, were precise. Tim caught Churchill's strengths and weaknesses, his self-assurance and doubt, his confidence and petulance, to perfection – a most splendid tour de force. So, now he would add Churchill to his *An Age of Kings* credits, and to his Siegfried, to his Dudley and to his Prince Albert, and so on.

He took on the Churchill persona again in *War and Remembrance* in 1988, a few years after *The Wilderness Years*. In a Miss Marple in 2006 again he played the part, and in 2015 in 100 days that saved Britain. 'Filming was difficult and very tiring for 100 days,' Tim impressed upon me, 'We were filming in the small hours and in the tunnels of Dover Castle. I was exhausted after one particular session and made for a chair. Immediately an English Heritage hatchet-faced harridan leapt at me with all the ferocity you might expect from such a person. "You can't sit in that seat, it's being conserved!" "Well, my dear," I said to her as sweetly as I could, "I'm afraid that this actor is in far greater need of conservation." And with that I planted my bottom firmly on the chair.' At 89, I think Tim deserved the use of any chair in the small hours of the morning.

On the stage, he memorably played Churchill in a French play about de Gaulle: *De Gaulle Celui qui a dit non* in Paris and, much more recently, but briefly, he played the man again in *The Audience* by Peter Morgan, at the Gielgud Theatre. Sadly, a fall caused him to withdraw, but I never thought it was quite the play for him.

Tim would often appear, when asked, to read a letter or two from the vast correspondence between Churchill and Clemmie, or perhaps one or two of Churchill's memorable wartime speeches. He found it hard to refuse and, I believe, looked on this sort of thing almost as a duty.

Celia Sandys, granddaughter of Sir Winston, is the daughter of Duncan Sandys and Diana, Churchill's eldest daughter (1909-1963). She is the youngest of three children – Julian (1936-1997), Edwina, Celia. Celia tells me:

'Tim first came into my life in 1984 when I raised the idea with my sister, Edwina, of a musical about our grandfather. It was really a 'throwaway' line, but she grabbed at it and in no time, we were in discussions with the director, Robin Hardy (no relation of Tim's but the director, I seem to remember, of *The Wicker Man*) and the producer, Rex Berry. They were very enthusiastic and cast Tim as WSC and Virginia McKenna as Clementine. Sadly, *Winnie* ran for only a few weeks, not because it wasn't good but because the necessary financing had not been put in place.'

Lesley Duff also starred in *Winnie* and has been a familiar face on television from *Wycliffe* to *The Bill,* from *Pie in the Sky* to *Taggart,* and so on. With Jean Diamond she founded, in

2013, what is now one of the most highly respected of the capital's theatrical agencies.

Lesley was cast in this little remembered musical – one of Tim's less successful ventures in the person of Churchill, though his portrayal was second to none, as always – alongside Tim and Virginia McKenna. Virginia admired Tim enormously and, is, perhaps, best known for *Born Free* and *Ring of Bright Water*, and her continuing work with the conservation of animals, a passion engendered by those films. Lesley adds to the general picture:

> 'Julien, I am very happy to respond. *Winnie* was an ill-fated show that opened in Manchester, then London in about 1988, and it was a constant struggle. Robert was brilliant, I found him tricky and incredibly funny, I became very fond of him and Virginia. We had so many laughs in the face of disaster!

Celia Sandys continues:

> 'Tim charmed me from our first meeting and was happy to come with me to Harrow for 'Churchill Songs'. He charmed the boys as well, and they greeted him with excitement either as the Winston Churchill they had seen in *The Wilderness Years* or as Siegfried from *All Creatures Great and Small*. This was the beginning of a lovely friendship that we both enjoyed for the next thirty years. Tim got on very

well with Ken Perkins whom I married the next year, and agreed to be godfather to our son, Alexander. He took his duties very seriously. After suggesting that the Christening should be in the Bath Chapel in Westminster Abbey, he moved on to a more worldly involvement. When he was very young, Alexander would follow him around with great devotion and then with huge excitement when Tim took him shooting rabbits with bows and arrows in the Savernake Forest, where we moved to in 1993. It became a tradition for Tim and my aunt, Mary Soames (1922-2014) to spend the New Year with us. But he was a frequent guest at all our houses as we moved from London to Berkshire, to Devon, and then to Wiltshire. I have so many happy memories of Tim and the fun and joy that he brought with him whenever he came to stay. Even simply walking in Marlborough with him as the shopkeepers greeted him. It did my 'street cred.' no end of good and I knew I'd get better service as a result! Choosing a godparent can be a hit or miss affair but if it works it is a great plus for a child to grow up and develop a friendship with someone of his parents' generation. Tim was the perfect choice. Not just in the early years but after Ken died, he became even closer to Alexander – always there to advise and listen. We were lucky to have him in our lives.

Tim agreed with alacrity when I suggested we might do a combined reading of my grandparents' letters at an International Churchill Society dinner at Blenheim. We spent quite some time choosing the material and had fun rehearsing it. It went down very well, and we repeated it in Winchester. We even planned to take it to America but, sadly, that never happened.'

Nigel Havers played Randolph Churchill in *The Wilderness Years*. Randolph had a difficult relationship with his father it is true to say, and this is shown very well in the series. But off the set, the relationship was very different and full of nonsense. Nigel continues:

'I remember filming *The Wilderness Years* with Tim – once, we were based in Phoenix, Arizona, for bizarre reasons that now escape me. We completed our last day of filming and Tim was determined to celebrate. He hired a car and booked the best restaurant in town. He was always the most generous of hosts and was most knowledgeable about wines and we made a large dent in the best corners of the cellar. When the time came to return to our hotel, Tim would brook no argument. He was determined to drive, despite being extremely 'merry'.

Off we set, Tim at the wheel, and half-way into our journey, he turned to the rest of us and said with a grin: 'See, I told you I was fit to drive.'

'Absolutely!' we chorused, 'you're driving beautifully, Tim, but maybe we should point out that we are still driving on the wrong bloody side of the road!'

Suffice to say, we made it to the hotel safely – somehow.

This is simply a tiny snapshot of someone with the biggest heart and an exuberant love of life. He is sadly missed.'

Emma and Justine – Tim's daughters – remember Tim's driving as a very serious affair, not to be taken lightly. And I, too, remember being driven most carefully when he thought it his turn to drive. However, I also recall how eager he was to be photographed in a pub car park pretending to get drunkenly into the driver's seat of my car holding a half-empty bottle of wine, just for sheer devilment.

We met James Murray earlier and learnt something of his friendship with Tim. It was a close relationship, and it became more so as Tim neared the end of his life. James kept alive Tim's interest by revisiting *The Wilderness Years* with a rather clever idea in the year before he died.

'We decided it would be fun to work on something together, and so we began to build a live audience question-and-answer show whereby I'd play the doting interviewer and Tim would play – well, Tim would play Robert Hardy talking about his time filming *The Wilderness Years* some thirty-five years earlier. (Around the time I was discovering the Hardy endorsed yew tree.) We had the good fortune to have months of rehearsal time to build the show, and I remember it being a very happy time for Tim. It was such a privilege to observe a talented man as he reminisced about his life. I absolutely relished it. Tim's mind was full to brimming with words, images, ideas, memories, imagination etc. and he had a unique ability to fuse all these qualities together to deliver them in a profoundly considered, yet light and humorous manner. I have yet to come across anyone else with such a remarkable skill as this.

By the time the show came round (at the Theatre Royal, Winchester) we could 'do it in our sleep.' What blew me away on the night was how this nonagenarian not only rose to the occasion (ninety minutes on stage) but positively glowed with pride and exuberance when discussing his work as Churchill. Tim answered questions from the audience with such wit, panache, and gusto that the mood had turned quite emotional by the time the curtain came down with plenty of glistening eyes out in the stalls, which, I imagine, was just how Tim had planned it!

I continued to spend time with Tim throughout the following months: there was a planned trip to Churchill's house at Chartwell, talk of a US tour of our show, and all manner of grand and ambitious ideas, which I think he would have embraced had it not been for his hastening age.

He would refer to this 'fly-in-the-ointment' as 'a real bugger, you know!'

So meticulous were Tim's preparations and attention to detail it is worth reminding readers that Tim persuaded Churchill's jeweller to make a replica of the great man's signet ring for his use whilst filming. Furthermore, Tim tracked Churchill's dentist and persuaded him to make an oral plate that would enable Tim properly to counterfeit Churchill's speech impediment. In 2015, Tim gave a lecture at Hillsdale College, Michigan on Churchill and on playing the part of Churchill. In the photograph of the occasion, Tim wears Churchill's spotted bow tie, sold at auction after Tim's death, for £5,000. At the same auction, the Churchill Stetson worn by Tim in the Theatre Royal production above, sold for £3,200.

# *All Creatures Great and Small*

Before filming the first series of *All Creatures Great and Small* the BBC declared most emphatically that Donald Sinclair – the model for Siegfried Farnon still practising as a vet in Thirsk at the time – was to be left alone and not contacted by anyone. Donald Sinclair was, therefore, 'forbidden territory'. Tim explained to me 'So I made an appointment to see him almost immediately, not because I was in the habit of being disobedient but because I simply wished to learn as much as possible about the man I was to portray.' Tim's eyes twinkled a bit with naughtiness when he disclosed this fact to me. Though Donald and he eventually became friends, Sinclair never took to Tim's

Siegfried even though (perhaps because of) Donald was far more eccentric than Tim's portrayal ever was.

The casting of Peter Davidson in the role of Siegfried's lazy, but charming younger brother, Tristan, in *All Creatures Great and Small*, brought him to everyone's attention. He was a clever choice and was involved with the serial for twelve years, fitting in two further popular series as *Dr Who*, the time-traveller and *Campion*, the Lagonda-driving detective. Since those days, his television and theatre diaries have remained full to bursting. Tim was very fond of him and thought highly of him as an actor always hungry to learn. Peter is delighted to share these amusing anecdotes:

'Well, it is no simple task to sum up a life in a few words, not least a life so full and distinguished as that of Timothy Sydney Robert Hardy CBE FSA, or Tim, to his friends and family and colleagues. One of those friends was Richard Burton whom Tim had known ever since Magdalen College, Oxford, in the 1940s. Their friendship continued through the beginnings of their acting careers until Burton's death in 1984. The friendship even survived Elizabeth Taylor. Tim himself began his career in 1949, and throughout the 50s his star rose, with leading roles at Stratford and the National Theatre. I wish I could say that I had been there, and seen him on stage in those days, but, alas, I was four years old at the time and not quite tuned in to the joys of Shakespeare. The same did not apply to other members of my family.

I first met Robert Hardy in the early summer of 1977, when the cast of *All Creatures Great and Small* was gathered in a small hospitality room at the BBC Television Centre. The meeting was problematic for me because I vividly remembered the first time I had seen him on the telly, seventeen years before, in 1960, in the BBC's *An Age of Kings*. And we had watched it, not because it was cast with the finest in British theatre, but principally it was obvious my mother had a huge crush on the actor playing Prince Hal. And why not? He was dashing, handsome and sexy and he had the coolest haircut ever. Perhaps all that is why, a few years later, I did my best to copy his Prince Hal soliloquy to scrape myself into drama school.

Now here I was, seven years after that, cast to play his younger brother, and meeting him face to face for the first time. I had been told that while, to his friends he was Tim, you could not address him as such, but rather had to wait until invited to do so. I was dry-mouthed with nervousness, insecure about my south London vowels, and slightly panicked because the first thing Christopher Timothy [James Herriot] had just said to me, rather too loudly, was

'Too tall, recast!' The first thing I remember Robert Hardy saying to me was 'Call me Tim!'.

When I told my mother I had a part in *All Creatures Great and Small* she said, 'That's nice, dear.' However, when I told her I was playing Robert Hardy's brother, she was breathless with excitement. Over the next few months and eventually over the next twelve years, he became a major influence in my life.

As we rehearsed, I'd watch him carefully. Even scenes I wasn't in, I would stand and gaze in admiration, and in the end, I think it 'creeped him out' (as he most certainly would not have said!). One day he came over and said cheerfully but challengingly 'Why are you watching me all the time?' 'I'm your brother' I replied. The truth was I was mesmerized. In rehearsal, and on camera, I never saw a scene in which he did not sparkle like a diamond. Whilst I would edge towards a dreary honed consistency, he was too excited by the infinite ways a scene might be played. It had its downside of course: some of his most brilliant performances were only seen in the Acton rehearsal rooms, and when it didn't go quite so well on camera, he would be angry with himself, and perhaps sometimes the ripples of his self-reproach would spread outwards to those around him.

We bonded best in the scenes we had together – just the two of us. They were usually confrontational, highly charged and, I hope, amusing. I learned quickly to expect the unexpected. Sometimes he would bark lines at me, sometimes hiss them with barely controlled fury, sometimes gesticulate wildly, sometimes remain calm and angelic. When we ran the scene again, it was all entirely different. It was intoxicating, liberating; and while I could never hope to match him, I gave it my best shot. We both loved those scenes, and he grew to forgive those dodgy vowels, gently corrected my pronunciations, and was always relentlessly supportive and encouraging.

He was always amused that his severest critic was his dog, a whippet named Christie. On studio days he would bring the dog to Birmingham where he would play one of the Skeldale House dogs. He would sit quietly and faithfully on set, there on the living room sofa, while they rolled the tape and gave us our cue. All would go swimmingly until Tim began to act. That was Christie's cue to slide off the sofa and discreetly leave the room.

Sadly, I couldn't say that we were able to remain close friends in this odd, transitory, ephemeral world of ours, this make-believe. We all have the best of intentions but so often we move on to new adventures. And perhaps I was too much in awe of him, of his unique acting talent, of his prodigious knowledge in all things, and his elegant use of language. But he offered me the hand of friendship in those important years, and for that I shall always remain grateful. He played me his favourite music on drives up to Yorkshire and introduced me to a particular brand of whisky on freezing-cold hillsides once we'd got there. Once, we shared a pot of the finest Royal Beluga caviar. I remained unconvinced. If we were talking cricket, Tim would be of the 'Gentlemen' and the rest of us merely 'Players'.

Yes, I owe him so much, perhaps, even, my entire career. I might have been in only a few episodes if Tim hadn't demanded more scenes with the two brothers, because he felt they worked so well. And along the way he taught me the joy of playing those scenes rather than the relief of just getting through them. And he had moments of more dubious generosity too. In one of the episodes, I remember with fondness the artificial insemination collection sequence. My character was supposed to be standing idly back while the expert Siegfried showed Tristan how it was done. The show's vet adviser, Jack Watkinson, ever authentic and practical, had set up the real thing, and was explaining to Tim the methodology of getting between the bull and the cow, large test-tube in hand, at the exact moment the one mounted the other. 'Precision is everything' I heard Jack say, 'otherwise things can get a bit messy!' I could see Tim considering the full impact of this information and watched his brow furrow as he walked slowly over to the director. With an unexpected burst of enthusiasm, he said 'Do you know, I think it would be a much funnier scene if I instructed Tristan in what he should do and let him get on with it.'

He became an actor, he said, because he loved being other people. He liked to get to know them, the way they thought, what drove them onwards. That, he said, was the joy of it. I know exactly what he meant.

After three series, we went our different ways – for a while. I went off to do *Doctor Who*. (Incidentally, I rang him up for advice when I was offered that part, and he told me not to touch it with a barge pole. Well, he may well have been right.) Tim went off to play Churchill in *The Wilderness Years*. He was brilliant of course. He was Churchill. He insisted later that he hadn't wanted to do it, and that he had suggested other actors, but I am pretty sure he knew he was born to play the part. He did it so well that when we reconvened to do more of *All Creatures*, a couple of years later, we all noted there was now more than a little Churchillian influence in the character of Siegfried! Of course. he did so much more than *All Creatures Great and Small*, and Churchill, though he played him many times: from Henry V through to Cornelius Fudge in the Harry Potter series, with Mussolini, Malcolm Campbell and Prince Albert, and many other roles, in between. And alongside all that, he managed to bring up a family, and dedicate fifty years to his passion for the longbow. Even so, I like to think his time on our little vet series was one of his happiest. We were like a family. I talked to Carol Drinkwater, the first Helen Alderson/Herriot, just after Tim's death: she felt his passing had left a bigger void than she could have imagined. So, thank you, Tim, whether you like it or not, you were my mentor and inspiration.

Postscript: I last saw Tim in October 2016 when Christopher Timothy, Carol, Tim and myself attended a dinner in Yorkshire to celebrate James Herriot's centenary. I hadn't seen him for many years – far too long. He carried a walking stick now, but, apart from that, seemed as sprightly as ever. Many years before, sometime towards the end of the first series, he told me he'd like, one day, to direct me in *Hamlet*. I wasn't quite sure if he was serious, or if it was just his way of saying that I was doing okay. But the following year he asked me again but playing Hamlet was too frightening to contemplate, and I'm afraid I dodged and deflected. He didn't give up asking – maybe two or three times after that. I am ashamed to say that I never said, yes. Now here we were again. He was 91 and I, 65. It seemed a good day to explain myself. Halfway through the evening, I crouched beside him and said how much I regretted my years of prevarication, and how sorry I was I'd never let him direct me in Hamlet. He turned to me, quick as a whippet, and, grabbing my wrist, with a twinkle of excitement in his eye, 'Well,' he said, 'We must do it now!''

Tim with Peter Davison

# Sense and Sensibility

In 1995, *Sense and Sensibility* was done and dusted and released the following year. What pure gold it is in its remastered DVD. The screenplay is by Emma Thompson's hand, and she also plays the part of Elinor Dashwood so beautifully. Emma does no violence to Jane Austen's novel, but brings certain aspects into sharper focus, and allows the story to be better balanced as a two-hour film. Ang Lee (*Crouching Tiger, Hidden Dragon* 2000 and *Life of Pi* 2012) filming his first English novel directs with good sense and sensitivity. In fact, more than that, he applies a golden touch to the whole. And there could not have been a better cast – Kate Winslet, Alan Rickman with his disciplined and restrained passion, the diffident goodness of Hugh Grant's Edward, and the most amusing but barely controlled Hugh Laurie exasperated by his wife's constant prattle. Much could be written in praise of each, and every one.

The widower Sir John Middleton is a gem of a part for Tim, so cleverly coupled with Elizabeth Spriggs' Mrs Jennings, his mother-in-law. Sir John is a generous benefactor and a man who sees the pleasure, beauty, and fun in the world around him. He loves his friends and family, leg-pulling, gentle mockery, raucous laughter, giggling with his mother-in-law, his six assorted wayward dogs, with not a whippet among them.

He plays this larger-than life, ebullient personality with aplomb and ease. He is, perhaps, a Sir John Falstaff sans melancholy and vulgarity! Tim is in his element, drawing heavily upon and tapping that seam in his own character. He is an absolute joy to watch, especially when he guffaws, sniggers and giggles away with Elizabeth Spriggs. Of course, those guffaws, sniggers and giggles continued 'off camera' as well, you can be sure.

It was while filming *Sense and Sensibility* that Tim first stayed at Plumber Manor, where he subsequently enjoyed a brief encounter and love-affair with the lawnmower. At the time, Tim had just sold Upper Bolney and was about to begin his Scottish adventure at Newhall. Some years later, after visiting the cinema, Tim wrote to Ang Lee praising his work on *Sense and Sensibility* and his subsequent films. (And this is interesting. Tim always was anxious to give praise and credit when and where they were due, and frequently did so. Interviewers were often at pains to goad their subject into saying something that could easily be turned into a less pleasant, derogatory, or acerbic comment by the stroke of a malicious pen. Why, I wonder? The fact is that Tim greatly respected his fellows and marvelled at and enjoyed skill that was revealed in any field.) In response to Tim's letter, Ang Lee sent a handwritten reply in thanks for the congratulatory remarks. He tells Tim that the letter warmed his heart, 'brought back great memories of making *Sense and Sensibility*' and 'brought smiles on my face'.

I once remember saying: "ere 'Ardy, you was at your ebullient best in that film, you was a veri'able ebullient cove. I really enjoyed it.'

'Yeah' he agreed, maintaining the questionable 'cockney' and the nonsense. 'I was, as you so rightly say, I was wonderfully ebullient.' He grinned and his eyes glinted. 'By the way, what is ebullient? Is it somefing for bad backs, I wonders, like an embarkation?'

# The Shooting Party

I mentioned in the opening chapter that one of Tim's stories on that first luncheon encounter, was the account of the hideous crash at the start of filming *The Shooting Party*. I heard it many times later, but it didn't seem to vary in any way.

'Well, the crash, yes. It was certainly nightmarish.'

'This was in the grounds of Knebworth.'

'Indeed, most of the filming took place there – inside and out. Anyway, there were six of us, I think, in the wagonette-break, which I believe it was.' Tim was picturing the scene as he had done many times since the event. 'It was drawn by two greys in pole gear, the driver, a vastly experienced man. We set off as soon as "*Action!*" was heard. It was as though the clutch had been let in rather too enthusiastically. The horses may have already been spooked by something. So, there we were, off at a fair lick. Something wasn't right, though. Perhaps I didn't know that at the time. Difficult to put a finger on it. But we were travelling fast – rather too fast for comfort. Then suddenly, the footplate came adrift and dropped down – and poor old George followed still clutching the reins.' Tim's excitement was palpable, and he held up his left hand as though the tale still astonished him. In doing so, he only narrowly avoided a rather serious molestation complaint from the waitress, who had appeared quietly and dutifully at his side. We ordered and the Chablis arrived. I waited as Tim instructed the wine waiter that the wine needed only to be chilled, not frozen to death.

'And then?' I asked anxious for more horror, having suddenly acquired the taste for it from Tim's narrative.

'Oh, Yah, the chariot run. Well, it was, for a moment, almost farcical because it seemed as though another hand had sped us up to a pace that was well-nigh impossible.'

'Like the film speed of the Ben Hur chariots.'

'Exactly! With the disappearance of the driver, George…no, he was actually seen, briefly, underneath the wagon and then spewed out behind. By now he had let go the reins. The reins were loose underneath the wagon and the desperate cries of 'Whoa!' and 'Stop!' from the passengers, unsurprisingly proved ineffective. The horses were now terrified, and their heads tossed about, and their ears flicked alarmingly back and forward. Suddenly they caught sight of a huge tree ahead and that seemed to check their speed for a second or two. At that point two decided to leave the vehicle with a Geronimo! leap. I think one hurt himself, the other did not. The next thing I can recall is a stone wall looming before us as I thought, *O Hell! What now?* But the wall caused the horses to swerve violently to the right; the wagon twisted off the ground and seemed to snake about above the ground in slow motion, sending its contents – us – through the air with some considerable velocity. We came to rest against and amongst the spare and unused tubular steel fence propped beside the fence proper, as though we had simply been spat out. Silence!'

Tim's left hand was raised again but this time he looked about to ensure there could be no accusation of interference with the serving staff. 'I must be badly injured, I thought. I patted myself. No. I got up with a slight wobble extracting myself from the tubing. Paul [Schofield] was in a bad way with a shin bone protruding through a sock, muttering over and over again, 'This is crazy'. But Edward [Fox] was on his feet. Good, he's standing so must be alright, whereupon he turned green, dropped to the ground and was a goner for a few minutes.' Tim grinned but immediately checked his relish and tempered his grin. 'I began to walk back up towards what appeared to be a huge crowd of actors, crew and so forth coming towards us.' He beamed. 'And that is why Paul was replaced by James Mason. It was, of course, Mason's very last film. And, by the way, I understood later that the insurance representatives arrived before the ambulance. When we did get around to filming the start, we arrived safely in a motorised shooting break without a horse in sight.'

✳✳✳

The film itself is a beautifully made film of mostly two-dimensional characters, all known to each other with no time to develop in front of the audience. It is a snapshot of England on the eve of the First World War and, yes, it reminds us that many things were about to change. (Not that they changed as much as one might be led to believe.) But is that really what the film is all about? It always seems to me to be a tableau of human frailties - and we have them all paraded before us – in the context of the Shooting Party, of landowner, his acquaintances, and those more or less content to be employed on the estate.

There is no social comment on what is before us. Society has reached a certain point and things are about to be changed or modified because of the war. However, what is actually going to happen is that this assembly of human frailty will either translate to France or remain in England bereft of those who are now abroad. The new circumstances may correct, help them overcome, or exacerbate these frailties. Circumstances may strengthen them or crush them or do very little to change them at all! The film-goer may see in the film many different strands, and there can be no 'correct' interpretation.

Leaving all that aside, what about the acting? The acting is the true winner here along with the house itself. What an incredible ensemble, perhaps one akin to that required for an early Haydn symphony. The oboist has no interest in blowing a trumpet and the violinist is content to remain with the strings. Gielgud plays his eccentric part, but no one cowers before him. Tim underplays his silly, vulnerable character cleverly and allows his wife to shine, as does James Mason, but in a rather different way. Fox's disgrace is beautifully portrayed, and yet he doesn't overshadow anyone. And Gordon Jackson could have stolen the final scene but did not because there was no need to. In playing this ensemble piece so well, so unselfishly, this group of actors proved itself to be a group of true masters of the stage.

To return briefly to the 'meaning' of the film if, indeed, one is to be searched for, perhaps one might view the Mason/Jackson scene as representative of the reconciliation between God and man. Mason can be seen as a Godlike 'type' in the film, and Jackson is a likeable but worthless and notorious poacher despised by estate worker and others. And yet, it is landowner Mason who will hold the hand of the dying poacher and pray with him the paternoster.

Lord Cobbold, at the time of the filming of *The Shooting Party*, was heir to the barony and Knebworth, and was content, nay, thrilled to be employed as a third or fourth-string 'run-about' for the crew: his tasks ranged from carrying messages here there and everywhere to early morning ice-breaking on the Lake, trying to pretend the time of year was, in fact, autumn rather than a freezing winter. Recalling these months, he continues:

'Julien, I have extremely fond memories of Robert Hardy on the set of *The Shooting Party*. It was my first job out of college, so I was very much a minnow in the pond – despite my home, Knebworth House, being the location. However, this unique shoal of actors made the whole experience feel very egalitarian and feel more like a party. I recall the Green Room being a salon of anecdotes and stories – Gordon Jackson, Frank Windsor, Dorothy Tutin, Robert Hardy – and it was, quite simply, the all-time fantasy dinner guest list. But this was not a weekend party at my house, this was the whole autumn at my house!

Company aside, it was not a trouble-free shoot. The film was set over three days, much of it 'exteriors' so keeping weather continuity was a problem and there were delays. These delays, of course, meant more time for stories in the Green Room – wonderful for a young film student, less good for the producers and the bond company. Robert Hardy, I remember, maintained his good humour and bonhomie throughout. Of all the cast, he was the most interested in Knebworth House and its history. My overriding impression was of a man who had an interest in all things. In the film, his character's defining line is that he doesn't think he would want to know people he had nothing in common with – I cannot think of a line more unlike the real Robert Hardy!'

# Castles in the Air

Newhall House, Midlothian, Scotland

In this chapter, we shall visit the castles Stephen Weeks will mention while filming his first attempt at *Gawain and the Green Knight*. And we shall also become acquainted with Tim's less-than-successful and short-lived encounter with his own Scottish castle. Stephen is a writer, director, and conservationist. He began his professional career as a director at the tender age of seventeen, with his first cinema film, *1917*, when he was twenty years old. At twenty-three, his third film was *Sir Gawain and the Green Knight*, with Tim in the role of Sir Bertilak. He remade the film in his early thirties as *Sword of the Valiant*, with Sir Sean Connery. After this, he was making *The Bengal Lancers* in India when the film was halted by a huge insurance fraud. It took many years to piece together what happened, and to believe that a well-known laboratory was part of the fraud.

Stephen then turned to his other love - restoring castles - and in 2003 moved from Wales to Bohemia where he has been involved in that type of conservation work, as well as writing. His novels - popular in the very best sense - include the ingenious and splendidly researched detective series *The Countess of Prague*. One of his most recent books is *The Pain of Mrs Winterton*. Stephen kindly provides the following entertaining sketches of his various encounters with Tim.

'I was twenty-three and setting up my third film – an adaptation of the medieval poem, 'Sir Gawain and the Green Knight'. It was 1971. It seemed natural if I was to recreate the Middle Ages, then Robert Hardy should play in it – especially as there was a character called Sir Bertilak, lord of the hunting castle. We would shoot in the autumn and winter. (At the moment of casting it was high summer.) A meeting had been arranged, and I was asked to drive out to Tim's home, Upper Bolney House, near Henley-on-Thames.

Everything was perfect. Up the gravel driveway in the rolling countryside, the house was glorious – timber framed, thatched, if I remember correctly. His interiors – the furnishings and paintings – could have been assembled from an old collection. It was all so quintessentially English, just with a touch of film glamour – the kind of thing that some Hollywood magnate might have moved complete, timber by timber, to Beverly Hills!

We had drinks on a terrace near the tennis court. And Tim was charming, properly theatrical, and full of information about so many aspects of medieval life; we could have talked for hours. (At Oxford, studying English at Magdalen, he had been a student of C S Lewis…Wow! I came away with my head spinning. And now I had an actor, the actor to play my Sir Bertilak.)

There was a costume fitting at Bermans and Nathans, and Shura Cohen, the costume designer, had found in the stock collection, the original cloak worn by Sir Laurence Olivier in Henry V – the King's heraldic cloak, made in 1944. Olivier's name was written on a piece of paper pinned to the collar. It naturally suited Tim, who even gave us a flash of that famous speech before Harfleur.

Making the film was quite arduous, although Wales looks quite romantic in the mist and gloom of late autumn and winter, it doesn't feel quite so romantic at the time! Tim's character, Sir Bertilak, had his own special castle, Castell Coch, just north of Cardiff, a border castle restored to perfection by the gothic revival architect, William Burges, for the 3rd Marquess of Bute in the 1880s. (Burges's own gothic house, in Melbury Road, Kensington, was bought and lived in by Richard Harris, after he had become besotted with all things chivalric after starring in *Camelot*.) Coch has a working drawbridge and portcullis, beautifully counterbalanced.

Tim's first scene was in the great hall. It is just dawn outside, and, inside, the courtiers are mostly asleep on their benches, with the wine jugs still on the tables. Young, dishevelled, ragged Gawain is led in by the castle porter – but he is still able to project himself as a knight. Sir Bertilak, on his high seat, is awakened. Yawning, he steps forward into the gloom. 'Open those shutters there,' he orders, pointing to the shuttered windows. The shutters creak open, and early morning sunlight floods in. By 'sunlight' I mean two five-kilowatt lamps somehow suspended on the castle wall outside – a feat that had taxed the riggers since there was a hundred-foot drop on that side of the building. So, the light floods in, Sir Bertilak walks across to Gawain, unfastens his cloak (the aforementioned cloak) and swings it over Gawain.

On any film set there are always catchphrases. No one can guess them in advance, but then they literally grab hold of the crew. Thus, it was that 'Open those shutters there' caught on and all the crew and cast members would use it whenever it was appropriate – or inappropriate. It was the way Tim had delivered those four ordinary words. He had plenty of other speeches, but it was those words which were soon on everyone's lips. Tim went on to do more scenes in Cardiff Castle – dreamy rooms atop towers also built by Lord Bute with William Burges at the helm.

There remained only one scene for him to do – in the hall of Fortinbras Castle, challenging its terrifying lord. However, tragedy struck. Tim, while we were working, asked the wrangler if he could ride one of the horses one afternoon. Naturally he was a good horseman, and usually film-trained horses are as tame as you like, except this one. It threw Tim into the dry moat of Castle Coch, and he sustained a broken pelvis.

At another Victorian fantasy, Peckforton Castle in Cheshire, we had created our Fortinbras. Sir Bertilak was supposed to stride in and confront Baron Fortinbras. 'I've come not to dally with you,' was the line. No striding for Tim, so we employed a local extra and shot on his back. Then we'd cut round to a close shot of Sir Bertilak sitting in an unseen wheelchair. Everything is set up and our local lad strides in and opens his mouth, ' I cum not t'dally with thee,' in as Cheshire an accent as was ever heard; the camera on Baron

Fortinbras and his heavyweights to catch their aggressive faces. Instead, the camera catches a group of actors falling about with laughter! Luckily, the reverse on the real Tim worked, wheelchair out of shot.

However, it was a few months after this incident that we got to post-synching. The original line, 'Open those shutters there' was not so clear on the original recording, because Tim was walking forward, pointing, and heaving his heavy cloak from his shoulders. By now, this was the classic line of the film, and everybody had connected to the film's catchphrase. I remember the film editor saying it before switching the light back on in the cutting room, for example. Tim was now on crutches, but much of the last months had been spent in a wheelchair, and now his voice was completely different. It wouldn't have mattered in normal circumstances, but these were not normal circumstances. We spent an entire session – four solid hours – trying that line over and over, and even Tim knew it wasn't coming out with the magic touch of the original. Eventually we had to settle for one, but all of us knew it wasn't *the one.*

I kept in touch with Tim, but my career with its few movies never was able to catch him again, but in the late seventies, he visited the 12th century castle in Wales I had bought as a ruin, and he enjoyed a thorough exploration of it. He showed me how to clean old oil paintings by carefully rubbing a brandy-soaked cloth over it, and how to get rid of stains on a polished table with lemon juice.

A year or two after, he invited me down to Henley-on-Thames again as he said he had something interesting to show me. He took me down to the cellar where there were many wooden bows, some of them strung. 'These were recovered from the wreck of the Mary Rose,' he explained. They had been at the bottom of the Solent since the mid-sixteenth century, and yet – as he demonstrated – the yew wood was still able to flex, and they were still excellent bows. He gave me a copy of his classic text on the English longbow. He was certainly no dabbling amateur; he had become the country's foremost expert on the subject.

I got Tim to voice a documentary I made on the vestiges of the battlefields of the Western Front in France and Belgium. *Scars* it was called, and it was ITV's Remembrance Day documentary for 1979. Tim's solemn and sometimes ironic reading was just perfect, and helped it win a couple of awards. I just wished I could have used him more.

We were not in touch again – apart from the usual exchange of Christmas cards and occasional correspondence – until the mid-nineties. In 1995, Tim had inherited an estate in Scotland – Newhall in the Pentland Hills. This was the culmination of a lifelong dream for Tim – to be a proper country gentleman, a real squire – just as he had played from time to time as an actor. The problem was that it was just too late in his life. The house needed a lot of work, all thirty rooms of it, and the park needed just as much. I was asked to visit as I had become something of an expert at getting country houses to work both architecturally and in terms of paying their keep by discreet tourism.

It was certainly an archetypal house in the Scottish baronial style with two circular turrets with conical roofs, seventeenth-century crow-stepped gables and a large gothic-style conservatory. Tim had been holed up there with Neil helping to keep the whole place from freezing. But what's a few degrees of chill when one has a history that begins as the site of a Cistercian monastery in the tenth or eleventh century? However, my visit occurred when the temperature was somewhat milder. Peacocks strutted on the lawn and at night their cries sounded like babies being murdered! Tim showed me round. 'This room will be my bow room.' He said 'I've got thirty wonderful specimens.' And he spoke of the gentlemanly pursuits the place afforded – hunting, fishing, riding, most of which I couldn't see him getting round to as clearly supervising plumbers and getting deer fences mended would probably consume most of the time.

At the time I had a connection to the Marquess of Linlithgow, Adrian, who lived about an hour away in the gargantuan Hopetoun House, a true palace that was one of Scotland's greatest country houses. Luckily, he also had the acres to sustain his pile in proper order. What Tim, Neil, and his house guests at the time – Emma Thompson and her husband, Greg Wise - did not know, was that I had recently played a practical joke on Adrian. I had made up a convincing fax as if from the Inspector of Taxes which suggested that as he claimed the proper expenses of a Marquess off his tax bill, then the said inspector would call for lunch, just to check he was indeed doing the things properly. The fax had fooled Adrian's secretary and had been rushed over to him as he was somewhere else on the estate. It took him two or three readings to realize the hoax. By the fourth reading he realized it just had to have been sent by me.

When we arrived at Hopetoun for our invitation dinner, after the long drive through dark trees and out on to the gravelled forecourt, the house was in darkness. The entire façade loomed up, black against the slightly light night sky. We pressed a doorbell. It rang somewhere distant. Then, after an extraordinary delay, right at the top of the house one light came on. The light moved to a lower floor, then again. At length there was a rattling of bolts at the door. The door opened, and there was Adrian yawning, and wearing a dressing gown. (I did not look to see if he was wearing monogrammed bedroom slippers.) Whoops! We must have got the wrong date. It was an awkward moment until Adrian suddenly removed his dressing gown to reveal that he was fully dressed and began to laugh. He'd got his own back.

We had a jolly evening and were well fed. When it was time to leave, Adrian apologized that a key member of staff was on holiday but that it was terribly easy for us to let ourselves out, just two floors below. However, there was a burglar alarm, and we were warned not to open the door catch before pressing the button or some such. Yes, it was terribly simple, so simple that none of us bothered to take it in. Also, humans always have a tendency to do exactly what we are told not to do. Five minutes later we were indeed stepping back on the gravel and just getting into the car when all hell broke loose – bells, sirens, searchlights. We decided to leave, and fast. As we were travelling down the drive, we saw the lights of a car coming towards us. Then the blue flashing started on top of it. The police blocked our escape. We all sat guiltily in our seats as the constable came over to us brandishing his torch. He peered inside. I was trying to think what to say, but it looked as if we should have to return to the house, and we should all waste a great deal of time. Maybe we'd be tested for alcohol, O Lord! Then the policeman spoke, his face creasing into what passed for a smile. 'Aha' he said, *All Creatures Great and Small.* In one minute, we were on our way again. Bedlam still raged behind us.

I did help Tim by drawing an illustrated guide to his park and gardens with stops at the delightful walled garden to admire the sundial, various follies and statues as well as a grotto, in the hope that he could attract school parties or even some coach groups. The catchment area was not bad, as the house was only sixteen miles from Edinburgh, but I never found out how this went. I just felt that he had become too old for his dream, far from the vigorous man with his longbows of nearly twenty-five years earlier.'

What Stephen did not know was that Tim's health was deteriorating on account of the intestinal cancer soon to be diagnosed. He underwent a successful operation in Edinburgh and when reassured by the surgeon on 'coming to' that the inwards he no longer possessed were 'better in the bucket' he seized on the phrase and regaled everyone with it to his immense pleasure, even though one or two turned rather green at the thought. But he had to rest from acting for a spell and was rendered incapable of doing any physical work on the estate during this period. The entire burden fell upon Neil in the role of his secretary as factor of the estate, his own acting career 'on hold'. It became clear that the enterprise was doomed to failure because of the huge workload and ever-increasing debt. And so, Tim moved south to an estate house at Charlbury in Oxfordshire where he was able to recover something of his old strength. Stephen continues his recollections:

'Later, in the 1990s we came together to see if we could produce a TV series called *Great Dinner Parties of the World*. Tim had excellent connections and a great friend in Churchill's granddaughter, Celia Sandys. She really could get this project on to the islands of the wealthy or into their mansions in Paris, their chateaux, their yachts. It all augured well, and finance was looming as we moved past the millennium. However, when 9-11 struck, I dropped out of the project for several reasons, which I know upset Tim.

One way or another that was our last contact. I had finally decided that I did miss him a lot and that I should make my peace with him. I had a message ready to go to his agent, as I did not know his current address. It was then I heard the news on Radio 4 that he had died. I had been planning to see if he could come to Prague so that I could show him some intriguing medieval mysteries. But it was not to be. He was a very special person.

Newhall had connections with the Scottish poet, Allan Ramsey (1684-1758), and, in the gardens, there is a sundial with the following inscription on it, somehow fitting for a man whose motto was to live every day as if it were his last:

"Observe how fast

Time hurries past,

Then use each hour,

While in your power;

For comes the sun,

But Time flies on,

Proceeding ever,

Returning never."

Perhaps it was slightly unkind of me to suggest that Newhall was a 'Castle in the air' as there were so many things militating against the success of the venture at the time. Tim, however, was not an easy person to dissuade from a course of action he had set his heart on, as Paul, his son, so rightly observed in an earlier chapter. He was also rather impetuous and would dive into an antique shop and buy something that had attracted him in the window, pay whatever was asked and leave happy and content.

Let us pursue the castle theme a little further before we conclude the chapter. Tim was not shy of admitting that he was always sensitive to atmospheres and memories, and sometimes ghostly sounds, immured in castles and ancient buildings. He also felt the horror of whatever had soaked into the fields of battle, both ancient and modern. Not all these things were terrifying to him; sometimes, quite the contrary. Indeed, at Newhall, there were occasions when he and Neil returned to the empty castle to hear the cheerful noise of a joyful gathering, a happy soirée coming from the rooms of the ground floor, a noise that ceased as soon as the main door was unlocked and unlatched. Just a fancy? I think not, as many genuinely seem more receptive than others to this sort of thing.

Perhaps it is, therefore, no surprise whatsoever that Tim embarked upon a short series of Castle Ghosts of England, Scotland, Wales, and Ireland for the Discovery Channel, in the late 90s. He presented the programmes live to camera, interviewed the witnesses, and gave the 'voice-over' commentary throughout. Amongst other places, he visited Muncaster Castle and the Tower of London; Glamis and Duntrune in Scotland; Carew and Gwydir Castles in Wales, and Huntington and Leap Castles in Ireland. All the ingredients are there to tickle the ghosthunter's fancy: Green Ladies, Grey Ladies and Phantom Pipers. The programmes are presented in Tim's customary authoritative and matter-of-fact manner.

The library at Newhall, reputedly Tim's favourite room

# Tim and the Family

## Paul and Sarah

I have already established that this book is not a conventional biography, and I shall not, therefore, be giving details of the lives and features of Tim's ancient ancestors by reproducing daguerreotypes and staid sepia photographs, nor the two fine 18th century portraits included in the final sale of Tim's effects, fascinating though that would be.

Tim was born in 1925 to Henry Hardy O.B.E. (a Rifle Brigade major and Headmaster of Cheltenham College and, later, Shrewsbury School) and Edith, the daughter of the Rector of Whitchurch in Shropshire, the Reverend Sydney Dugdale. Tim was the youngest of three sons – John, Richard and Timothy - and enjoyed or suffered, along with all youngest sons, both the pleasures and indignities of the role. I think his mother doted on him.

The current doings of his family were constantly on his tongue. His last remaining brother was poorly. His elder daughter, Emma, was in Brazil on a photographic assignment. His younger daughter, Justine, was in Tibet for a few weeks. His son, Paul, was moving house. So-and-so's marriage was in difficulties. So-and-so's partner was being difficult. He valued them all beyond price, got cross with them, was annoyed and exasperated by them, was sorry for them, loved them without reservation, and delighted in their company, and so on.

Tim's first marriage was to Elizabeth Fox, the daughter of Sir Lionel Fox. For some reason or other, it has often been reported that Elizabeth was a wardrobe mistress, a piece of nonsense that infuriated her. The marriage was fairly short, but produced Tim's son, Paul. Always, Tim was conscious of the fact that he was never a candidate for any 'father of the year award', and the reason for this saddened him. (It is interesting to note that in three of his best-known roles he portrayed a man who found it difficult to relate properly to a son or a younger brother – Prince Albert and his son the future Edward VII; Winston Churchill and his son, Randolph; Siegfried Farnon and his younger brother, Tristan.) In addition to this, he was aware of his general shortcomings as a husband. 'Good actor: bad husband!' he often admitted in interviews.

Tim's subsequent marriage to the costume designer, Sally Pearson, the daughter of Sir Neville Pearson and the actress, Dame Gladys Cooper, lasted much longer and produced Emma and Justine. All three children grew up in touch and as friends. Tim had four grandchildren.

We can gain a more personal glimpse of Tim, the family man, from members of his family, close and more distant. Unsurprisingly, his son, Paul, a respected and successful antiques collector and dealer in Somerset, has few memories of his father. Principal among them are the occasions when Tim 'sprang' him from school and lunched him thirty miles away in Winchester.

'I do remember that Dad…took me to the same hotel right in the heart of Winchester, and we always had Chateaubriand. Lord knows why we went so far: there must have been closer establishments of suitable quality for him, but he was a man who, once he had fixed on something, was rarely, if ever, dissuaded. This was in the early seventies when my hair was almost down to my waist, and school garb comprised loons and collarless cheesecloth shirts, with, maybe, an army greatcoat, if chilly. Lord knows what he made of it, in his tweed and moleskins. What a pair we must have been, in the splendour of whichever hotel it was. I wonder if he had an inkling then how important Winchester would become to him so many decades later.'

I recall one of my lunch trips to Oxford when I was expecting to eat locally, being required to drive to Stowe-in-the-Wold, to enjoy the creations of a Michelin Star chef! But I didn't mind in the least.

***

Always keen to seek out distant cousins and draw them into the framework and embrace of his immediate family circle, Tim became firm friends with the Bullen family distantly related through his maternal grandfather, the Shropshire parson. Inter alia, the family held Avington Park where Tim spent his last two years. Sarah, one of the six children of this internationally renowned eventing and show jumping family - Michael, Jane, and Jennie all represented Great Britain – lived with Tim and Sally and their daughters when a young aspiring actress. Sarah, noted as an actress and producer, became a familiar face on television. Many will remember her as the 'pin up', Operative Kate in *Space 1999*. She played Mrs Vasilakis in the Inspector Morse episode, 'Greeks bearing Gifts', and before that was seen in *The Sandbaggers*, and *The Fourth Protocol*. Sarah was Mrs Caradus in *House of Caradus*. Sarah is happy to admit:

'I owe Tim so much. He gave me my one and only stage make-up lesson by making my face up as 'a young thing' on one side and as an old woman on the other. He used to come round to Kennington and take me through my audition pieces when I was starting out. I particularly remember working on Chekhov and Strindberg – the trials and the tears – but he never stopped encouraging me. The family were very generous to me, and I virtually lived with them in the early seventies. It was at the time Tim was working on *All Creatures Great and Small* and he was also in the midst of extensive research and work with the longbows taken from the Mary Rose.

Sally was gloriously 'bohemian'. There was a time when we dressed up Justine as Sancho Panza, put her on the Hardy's donkey, whose name I cannot recall, and walked her solemnly down the hill to compete in the local fete as the 'Best Dressed'. Unfortunately, the time all this would take was not taken into consideration in the preparation, so that, by the time we arrived, this particular class was already over.

Tim and Sally were complete opposites; it was hardly surprising that they had the odd row. I particularly remember one incident when sitting having supper with them when suddenly there was an horrendous clattering emitting from the cupboard that held their cooking pots and pans. The culprit was one, Shreddie Baby, their pet polecat who had found his way into the back of the cupboard and was having a really jolly time making as much noise as possible. Tim hit the roof. (When his temper flared…well!) I seem to remember bowing my head and willing the storm to pass, and even clutching onto the table in case that vanished in the heat of the moment! In spite of the odd eruption, I can remember nothing but happy times spent with Tim, Sally, Emma and Justine. Indeed, Justine is a Godmother to our son, Edward. I was well aware that Tim could have his difficult moments, but I was devoted to him.'

Charlie, Sarah's brother, took on the running of Avington Park with his wife – another Sarah. She recalls:

'We did not see much of Tim until he left his Scottish castle behind and settled in Oxfordshire. On one visit we twisted his arm to open the Avington fete, resurrected after a gap of about fifteen years. We became good friends from that point. And he loved Avington, it was so gorgeous that he could come and spend his last years here with us. I think he was very happy – particularly with the views from his windows. We had great fun and laughed so much. He was wonderfully supportive of life at Avington and what Charlie and I were doing. Tim enjoyed reading the lessons at Evensong, and the church was always very full when he was on the rota! I remember that he willingly gave his time and signed endless autographs. He was a lovely man; we all miss him so much. We were so lucky to know him.'

# Elizabeth

Tim was godfather to his nephew, Henry - an Oxford academic and Sir Isaiah Berlin's principal editor - who treasures the delightful portrait of his mother Tim painted for him. She died in 1952 of poliomyelitis, when Henry was but three years old. Inevitably, Henry had only scant memories of her and asked his uncle to describe her. Tim responded with a piece that revealed his mother and, perhaps, something of himself. It is certainly worth including here and I am grateful to Henry for volunteering it.

EMMH – A memoir written for HRDH by TSRH

'Elizabeth came down the path from the top of the orchard, where I met her first with Rich, about where the upper lawn had been dug up to provide an air-raid shelter behind the almond tree. She was dark, and smart in her Wren uniform, dwarfed by Richard, who carried her suitcase. Rich was in the Army, a medical major, but I never remember seeing him in uniform. The story had it, and I think Richard never denied it, that he was in a pew behind her at St Mary's University Church in the High, and, gazing upon the nape of her neck, said to himself – that is the girl I shall marry. If true, I wonder whether the influence of Papa's fixation on a Ter Borch portrait of the back view of a woman playing the cello [*The Concert* c1675 Gerard ter Borch] had something to do with it.

There she was at all events, engaged to marry Richard, at Kingsland, which of course then was a purely private country house, to meet the family and be paraded for the first time. A tough experience in anybody's book, but she was cheerful, and had a smile in her rather lovely dark eyes, which I never saw desert them. Partly that smile was one of good nature, partly I think at the ordinariness, the mental slowness of life around her. There was in her an element of intellectual superiority, not altogether surprising in one who found herself in the bluff stupidity and discipline of the forces, and now thrust into a family such as she had not encountered before.

How did Rich win her? That is a conundrum; she ran rings around him in the speed of her thought; she was sharper, less gentle; but she acquiesced, and they became man and wife. Rich must have been persuasive and unyielding – the latter is a Dugdale trait. So one supposes he was driven both by desire and determination, and certainly love. He was a man whose fount of love was only ever surpassed by deep disappointment in the way the world went. But all that is much, much later.

Now, there was Elizabeth at Kingsland, feeling awkward but smiling secretly through it. Mama was welcoming and kind and understanding, all of which she often was, and she was sharp to detect unease, and to still it. Papa appeared rather aloof about it all and would refer to Elizabeth in her absence as 'the negress'. That I think to have been pure envy of her broad and well-formed mouth, as opposed to the thin lips all around him. I thought her mouth simply beautiful, and indeed was fascinated by her, always, and looking far back beyond that awful day, am still. Her informality probably irritated Papa. She came down to dinner the first evening in her WRNS white collar and tie with the regulation blue jersey over it. All very neat and delightful. Papa took exception and said that if she were to wear uniform at dinner, at least it might include the jacket. I told her the jersey was splendid, and asked if she could get me one, which she did, together with a naval belt, a fetching two-buckled affair, which I still possess, though the original jersey went long ago, to be replaced by many others. Looking back, I think she found me sort of OK, perhaps faintly amusing, being a mixture of shyness and an instinct to entertain. She was shy, but her driving intelligence and quick wit pierced through that to such an effect that the shyness was seldom obvious.

She would come to Kingsland on various leaves, until she became part of the family, always standing a little apart, as it were, but taking part in everything that went on with good grace, and often full of mischief.

We all drifted apart as the occasions of war led us, so there are not that many specific memories, until one particular day. I was in London, in uniform, and Elizabeth was either seconded or had been released by the Navy, to work for Sir John Maude, who was in some branch of Government, rather secret, I seem to remember. One day Elizabeth said, 'Come and see a film from Czechoslovakia, I think you'd enjoy it'. What her department had to do with secreted films from that part of the world I have quite forgotten, but we sat together, John Maude, Elizabeth and I, and Elizabeth was absolutely right, I loved it. It was all about knights and sieges and medieval warfare, and she knew that it would go down well with a romantic youth.

At all events, I used to see a lot of them during their young married life; at a flat somewhere near Haverstock Hill, where I stayed with them, off and on – Rich was soldiering and Elizabeth at the Department of Defence. All I remember was pleasantness, laughter, some expeditions to galleries or to the 'flicks' and the joy of being accepted, and with them. Later – how much later I don't know – I stayed at Boxmoor, when you and James were tiny. How close a mother she was I do not know, because she seemed apart from the squeals and smells of the nursery. I remember Mama, apropos the cost of that little house: 'Good Lord, it cost almost as much as we got for Aston'. (Aston had been sold in the early days of the war.)

This is all very scrappy, and wholly monocular, and I hope you grew to know Elizabeth soundly from your father. I was acting in the West End, with Sir John Gielgud in *Much Ado About Nothing* so it was in 1952 or 1953. [Palm Sunday 1952] I know Elizabeth was ill – Rich would ring me from time to time – and I knew it was a paralysis, but there was masses of it in London, and I thought at the worst she might emerge with a limp. I planned to go and see her. Rich rang to say that she had been put into an iron lung, and that was alarming. Saturday matinée, bright hot sunlight as I walked into the stage door at the Phoenix Theatre. The stage doorman, receiver to his ear, reached towards me through his little window and said 'Mr. 'Ardy, your brother on the telephone…good timing eh?' Never was worse timing; I took the receiver from the wall 'phone: Rich's quiet voice, under total control: 'I wanted you to be the first to know…Elizabeth died…' Silence, but the sound of the world crashing; what would become of Rich, of little Henry and James? It is only now that I think with a large gratitude that Rich wanted me to know so quickly because he knew that I was very fond of Elizabeth, and that we got on well, and sparked off each other quite satisfactorily.

I never stop thinking what it must be like for you and James, ever since that grievous day. I wonder so much what your memory, being the elder, is of her, is it too far away, and you too young, to be a reality? What it must have done to you both, and what remains of your wounds having your lives torn in half – no, more than half – like that. Her intellect, her intelligence lives on in you both. I only hope her sense of amusement at the world and its poor inhabitants lives on as well. With much love, Tim

Rich's second wife gave birth to two sons, the composer John, and Edward, now a priest at Pluscarden Abbey.

# Justine

Justine, Tim's younger daughter is, amongst other things, an author and a leading light in the admirable charity, Healing Kashmir, a mental health organisation helping those who are scarred and damaged by living in an environment of conflict and violence. There is no doubt Tim was immensely proud of her and her work. She tells me they enjoyed much nonsense together – the sort of cerebral nonsense he relished.

'Julien, yours has been such a juicy and merry friendship across the years, and the various projects. This was so much the marrow of Daddy, the combination of the joy of playing with language and the pleasure of another fine mind. As you know, he certainly did not suffer fools, but how he relished a good mind; indeed, as he did a good wine, and a well-made pork pie – these three being high on the list of his many joys. Daddy and I had such fun across the years, chatting away in accents and burrs from Donegal to Delhi, Peshawar, and on.'

I remember very well this skill of accents, burrs, and dialect. Once or twice, he enjoyed giving me one of his party-pieces of a conversation between a man from the south of Wales with one from the north, when I told him my Welsh accent always became distinctly Indian. (And along with a pork pie, he was extremely fond of 'damned good Scotch egg'.)

Justine has written movingly of her father's death. She was by his bedside for hours, along with Emma and Neil. Neil, who acted on four occasions with Tim in my adaptation of *The Dream of Gerontius*, was struck on several occasions during those vigil hours by memories of Tim as the dying Gerontius.

'When death is allowed to move at its own natural pace, it grants us one final privilege – to decide how we want to die. And yet, the shrill noise of fear can be so loud in the face

162

of death that it is easy for this final magnanimous gesture to slip past, unnoticed. TSRH did not miss it. He kept his archer's eye on its very particular target, one lid half closed to focus on this point of convergence. He was not pleased to find himself up against a foe that he could neither outwit nor defeat, particularly as he had danced such a successful jig around death's herald, the ageing process. He had always seemed years younger than his age, fooling us all that he had indeed made some pact with time. So, when time's arrows took the high ground, my father knew that he had been outmanoeuvred. Yet still he managed to charm The Dark Angel, even at the very end. As he had learnt from so many of his military heroes, he strategized. Perhaps he struck a deal, or simply used the steel of his own will, because my father died well, and entirely on his own terms.

If you want to maintain control over your treatment up to the very end, you have to prove to your doctor that you are still of sound mind. Dr Goodman was the gatekeeper of the mind in my father's case. He came to make one of these checks the day before my father died. At the sound of the good doctor's voice my father swam back up from the quiet place where he had been for several hours. His paling blue eyes opened, assessing who had come to disturb him. There it was again, that slight narrowing of the archer's eye. It is an expression wholly familiar to the residents of Skeldale House, to James and Helen Herriot, to beleaguer younger brother, Tristan Farnon, to the vast and heady cast of Harry Potter, and to every other film and television crew and audience book-ended in-between. That minute narrowing of the eyes carries an entire lexicon, ranging from an unspoken expletive to a schoolmasterly 'Are you absolutely sure that you want to say what you are about to say?' The words writ only in the flicker of a lid. It was an expression as familiar to us, his family, as it had been to the millions who have watched him across the seven decades of his career.

The good doctor put his head a little on one side. 'How are you?' he asked.

'How do you think I am?' It was hard to hear, the words barely surfing on the thinning thread of air.

'Do you understand why I have to ask the questions that I am about to ask you?' Dr Goodman continued.

My father's nostrils flickered, every movement however tiny, leaching from the last of the light.

The first few questions were as expected, name, date of birth, the date that day. Each was met with a whispered reply. They were basic questions assessing basic function.

Then the test for more complex thinking – the indirect question.

'What's your favourite university?' the doctor asked.

My father pressed his lips together. 'Durham!' The word shot out, clear and stronger than anything that had gone before.

'I thought you went to Oxford?' the doctor continued.

'Magdalen,' came another clarion answer.

The pale eyes were very wide now. One hand came from under the sheet to lift the other, the fingers still elegant even though his hands were made huge by the frailty of his arms, translucent, as though too much light from the summer garden beyond the window might shine right through them. One hand placed the other on the well-known chin.

'You asked which was my favourite university,' the words were precise. 'Which of my doctorates should I choose? Durham!' It was sharp, clear and once more he gave Dr Goodman the archer's eye. 'Wonderful city,' he said.

We hovered around the bed in the way of those who love around the fading beloved, every sense shuddering.

'Does irony count for mental clarity?' I asked the good doctor.

165

'I think so,' he smiled.

'Quite right,' came the fading voice, eyelids lowering, my father's face softening back into rest.

It was his last performance. It had all the power, wit, intolerance for perceived foolishness, and command of every other performance that my father had ever given. He underlined his legacy that one last time, at the absolute end of his lived life.'

During his final moments on 3rd August 2017, Neil emailed or texted me with the news and we agreed a prayer for Neil to say silently over him. A very sad task on my birthday but would Tim not have had a moment's joy in that knowledge? 'You'll always remember my Heavenly birthday, then!' I can imagine him saying those very words, grinning like a mischievous schoolboy.

# Emma

Tim's elder daughter is much admired for her photography and her father delighted in her international success in the field. She has been kind enough to allow me to include her memories and Justine's in the following affectionate sketch of life with their father.

'One of the compelling and recurring memories of my childhood is threading my way through our rose-filled garden, scattering the white fan-tailed doves feeding on the ground, on past tall hedges, tiptoeing alongside the vegetable patch with its rows of corn-on-the-cob reaching high over my head, and arriving at Dad's shed. We called it the archery shed, although he wrote there as well.

Opening the door, I was always enthralled by aromatic turpentine and beeswax, with an occasional top note of Gauloises. Dad might be there, working on a new longbow. Delicately curled shavings of yew wood, as fine and translucent as silk, lay at his feet, like confetti. He would show me a new bow end, carved from horn, or a jewel-like inlay of mother-of-pearl he had crafted into the bow handle, which gleamed iridescent.

As children, Paul Justine and I loved absorbing the careful beauty of it all, the elegant precision of the bow-making process, laid out in its various stages; his pens and ink, the piles of papers and writing, his beautiful writing, and scent of wood, of stillness, which I can recall without even closing my eyes. He kept his sitting room in the same almost hallowed fashion. The ends of his silk Persian rug were brushed straight – a ritual as we left the room – and we learned to help. How beautifully he laid a fire, rolling, twisting and knotting the newspaper so it looked like giant origami sea creatures. We copied him, hands darkened from newsprint. Sofa cushions were plump and smooth, he encouraged us to leave the room as we found it, in a reverential readiness. In the corner stood his beloved cabinet music centre where records were always dust free, and the needle always clean. I loved the amplified buzz as he removed a small ball of dust before setting the needle to play Sibelius, or Brahms, or Edith Piaf, Rachmaninov, Harry Belafonte, Songs from the Auvergne.

There was always, everywhere at home, a feeling of great respect, almost hallowed. It was important to do as he did, as much as we were able. He needed and demanded very high standards, in himself, and from those around him. Mediocrity was appalling to him. He carved a roast chicken like an artist; he drew like a draughtsman; he wrote like a calligraphist. He read us *The Lion The Witch and The Wardrobe* as I am sure C S Lewis – also his tutor in English at Oxford, by the way – would have wished it read. And as we all wept at Aslan's death, huddled on my little bed, Dad wept, perhaps most of all. And his use of language was always brilliant, rigorous, snazzy, inspiring. Well, elegance and precision in pretty much everything.

By the way, I have never met anyone who could drive with as much verve and accuracy combined. I remember how he changed lanes, driving fast without clipping the cats' eyes. In fact, he wagered a bet, the little bump of a cat's eye under his wheel merited a fine: sixpence in our hands. Neither Paul nor I found this a remotely lucrative pastime.

I don't think Dad was ever late for anyone, for anything, ever. Almost without exception, people recall encounters with him as utterly charming, captivating, elevating, inspiring, encouraging. Unless he decided someone was purposely foolish, or rude, in which case they would be dismissed, with a flourish and a flash of brimstone. Mostly though, he extended that fine quality of making people feel important; he listened with great focus; he drew out the best in people. We all wanted to please him because praise or attention from him felt euphoric. His concentration on perfection was awe-inspiring. Actually, a bit scary. He seemed God-like rather than human to me, as a child. I am sure he liked that very much and promoted it.

His temper was fast and fierce and all of us felt that fire, sometimes scorching hot. But when his kindly beam was on you, it was an intense experience, a warm and elevating light. Gruff and intimidating could revert to twinkly and elegant – Dad had immeasurable and far-reaching charm. Throughout my life people – friends and complete strangers alike – have told me, like a refrain, how Dad encouraged, supported, aided, and inspired them. He was certainly passionate and definitely romantic. It was his great pleasure to be among animals and trees, in the landscape, working with experts and artisans in those fields. He and my Mama kept dogs, horses, a donkey and pony for Justine and me, geese, and peacocks. He searched out the nobility in every

creature, horses especially. He adored them. Nobility drew
him in, fascinated him. And his love of ceremony, from the
everyday ritual of hand washing his bespoke wine glasses,
to the genuinely magnificent – such as reading the opening
to *Henry V* in Westminster Abbey on the anniversary of the
Battle of Agincourt – ceremony was oxygen to him, I think.
Medieval ceremony, pageantry, coats of arms, heraldry,
heritage, ancestry – these were captivating and irresistible,
and he wove them into his own fabric. And the history of
battles and weaponry, and struggle, and the romance of
great leaders, their charismatic impact. Perhaps a deep
longing of his was to be considered similarly.

In later years, when I had made a countryside home filled
with animals and trees and a vegetable garden with runner
beans that reached high over my head, he'd visit, and take
deep delight in everything. Justine called these years his
smiling Buddha years. He would sit at the head of the
kitchen table, laughing, always laughing, in a full throttle of
enjoyment, listening to his grandchildren. Then outside,
he'd show them how to pull a bow, or watch with pride as a
young horse was put through its paces. I think, alongside all
this, he sometimes wished for something greater, something
more, to keep improving, to stay curious, expansive,
immersed. It was not dissatisfaction; it was more like aiming

high and the opposite of complacency. (He would have loved a knighthood and it is wonderful that so many thought the same.)

His was a huge life, lived fully, passionately, with intent and intensity. I hope he rests knowing that his achievements were and are celebrated by thousands of thousands. It seemed, at times, as if he felt his life wasn't big enough for him. This upward energy he carried was inspiring and will be always. I am proud of where he set himself in the world; I am so proud that he was loved and cherished by so many. Dad was, and remains, an exceptional man. His life blood – his legacy - which we all carry: my siblings Paul and Justine, and our children – Alice, Sam, Robbie, and Cressida – is an essence of dignity, of elegance, of accuracy.

Back at the archery shed, Dad, like a magician artisan from a fairy tale, had wrapped and glued into place a dark green braid around the handle of an exquisitely small bow he had made for me, perfectly my five-year-old size. Outside, he showed me how to draw the bow, using his full-sized one. As he pulled back the bowstring, I watched his face, his eyes trained on his target, sharp, the nock of the arrow tucked to the right of his mouth, pursed in concentration, bracing the arrow on the string. It seemed to me that he aimed at the sun.'

# Neil

Neil with Tim and Justine

Inevitably, Neil features throughout this book, seldom taking centre stage, content, it seems, to carry spears and in that way generally support the principal action. But even that does not quite give us the actual picture.

Neil was born to an acting family. He has one brother. His father, Andrew Robertson, and his mother, Isobil Nisbet, were frequently seen on television in all the old favourites. Indeed, in the cinema, Andrew was seen in *Far from the Madding Crowd* (1967). Neil too appeared in that film but as a fairly new-born infant, and, consequently, had little memory of the casting.

Neil (always acting with the stage name, Neil Nisbet) had a busy and illustrious early career on television with many credits, including *Kids, Speed King* (BBC Playhouse), *Gulliver, The Brack Report, Claire, All Creatures Great and Small,* and *Trainer.* Notably, Neil acted with Tim, first, in *Speed King* in 1979. He brilliantly played the young Donald Campbell to Tim's Malcolm Campbell.

In 1990, after a few years in the theatre, both Neil and Tim's daughter, Emma, gained parts in an episode of *All Creatures Great and Small.* Being seen on horseback in this episode, stood Neil in good stead for the part he won in *Trainer.* At Barnwell Castle's Berenger Theatre in 1997, as a break from running Newhall, Tim played the Chorus and Neil the Dauphin in *Henry V.* and the following year Tim and Neil co-directed *Henry VIII* and played the Chorus and the Earl of Surrey respectively.

Between 2011 and 2013, Neil, as we have heard elsewhere, was the Guardian Angel to Tim's Gerontius on four occasions, in my adaptation of Newman's poem *The Dream of Gerontius,* for two actors, mezzo-soprano, choir and percussion. The venues were Beaulieu Abbey, The Oxford Oratory, Christchurch Cathedral, Oxford, and Winchester Cathedral.

In the early days, Neil would often stay with the Hardy family and at the time Sally, Tim's wife, left Upper Bolney, Tim

174

was employing a secretary and P.A. How, precisely, does Neil fit into the scheme of things? He became, to all intents and purposes, Tim's right hand and often, perhaps, a calming influence, with the ability to temper any over-enthusiasm Tim might indulge in from time to time, though not always. He was, first and foremost, Tim's godson but even that was not as straightforward as it might seem. Tim was certainly not in any way connected with the Robertsons at the time of Neil's Baptism so decided to 'adopt' Neil as his godson and forever refer to him as his godson.

And we know from Celia Sandys' experience (q.v.) with her son, Alexander, that Tim did not take on the role of godfather lightly – and, therefore, increasingly, responsibility would be coming his way. So, by the time the Scottish castle loomed on the horizon, Neil was rather destined to take on responsibility as its factor and keeper. With the move to Scotland, Neil increasingly performed many of the duties of personal assistant as his own career was put 'on hold'. As it turned out, this was around the time of Tim's illness and cancer operation, and so, inevitably, the full burden of the castle's upkeep fell upon Neil's shoulders. After only three years or so, with Tim's enforced convalescence and debt mounting by the minute as the castle soaked up money like a thirsty sponge, the estate house in

Charlbury, Oxfordshire, was found and the household removed to a less demanding place.

Tim increasingly relied upon Neil for day-to-day business, for diaries, appointments, travel arrangements, and so forth: it was a relationship beyond that of a close godson and a super-efficient personal assistant. Neil had by now become, in all but name, an adopted son. Of course, Neil knew the family well and was accepted as part of it; was never thought of as an employee but as a godson who gradually became a son. It is very difficult to put it in any other way.

At Charlbury, Tim settled in and continued his career – he was in Paris with the French play *De Gaulle Celui qui a dit non* in 1999 - and his involvement in his special interests with gusto. He began to work with Professor Matthew Strickland on what Professor Anne Curry refers to as 'The Longbow Bible' – From Hastings to the Mary Rose: The Great Warbow – published in 2005. Indeed, Tim didn't stop working –acting, writing and making 'appearances' - until he was over 91 and in his last few months.

Neil was understandably anxious to develop a second string to his bow and, with Tim's encouragement, began, in 2006, to work more regularly at Dragon Drama, a theatrical school for children and for young men and women. Both Tim and Judi Dench were enthusiastic patrons.

Neil's special character and good humour increasingly became powerful tools because as time went on, it was clear that a further move would soon be necessary and appropriate, and so the transfer to Tim's distant cousin's place at Avington, near Winchester, seemed right. The apartment at Avington was, of course, much smaller and Tim was certainly distressed to see much of his lifetime's collections of this, that and the other disappear under the auctioneer's hammer. Tim always admitted that he loved to be surrounded, as, indeed, I do, by what is commonly termed these days 'stuff' – books, objects of art and virtue, paintings. At Avington, Tim, still keen to work as hard as he could, loved the parkland, the views, and the local eating-houses, but, increasingly, Neil could detect that darker times were ahead. And the difficult final months involved not only the weaknesses that accompany old age but also the return of the cancer that had troubled Tim in the 1990s.

Though the family members were always involved, the immediate responsibility rested firmly on Neil's shoulders. He with customary good humour and unflagging generosity, nursed Tim until the final fortnight when twenty-four-hour medical care was desirable and necessary. However, we all know that the picture of Tim we all hold in our memories is a Tim of sparkling wit, bright eyes, mischievous eyes, the eyes of an erudite sage, the eyes of a naughty schoolboy! What tales can Neil tell us?

There are many hilarious episodes in which we can indulge ourselves, none more so than this little tale Neil told me amid fits of uncontrolled chuckles. I also received a useful contribution (another camera-angle, maybe?) of some vital statistics from the Richard of the story. I think Neil related this as we lunched not long after Tim's memorial service and I will now do my best to retell it:

The place was Plumber Manor in Sturminster Newton, that idyll of a place, a country house hotel owned by descendants of the man who built it early in the seventeenth century. Just Tim's cup of tea. He had first visited the place, I believe, when filming *Sense and Sensibility*, when he had made firm friends with the Prideaux-Brune family. On the day in question – the year was 1993 - Richard Prideaux-Brune ushered Tim and Neil with gentle ceremony into the garden to enjoy the evening sun after the car journey, and placed glasses of chilled Champagne into their hands. What more could anyone wish for? Having excused himself, Richard then began to mow the extensive lawns with a brand-new commercial-sized lawnmower – the sort of machine that would tackle a cricket ground without so much as a sigh. According to Richard, who spoke to me more recently, it really was a monster with an 850cc engine, quite an unwieldy machine to be controlled by a pedestrian. Richard, however, had mastered it and was proud of the fact and of the machine itself.

Our two spectator guests were now pleasantly settled with their second or third glass, though Tim could not keep his eyes off the lawnmower. He loved that sort of equipment. He was not going to be content to be inactive for much longer. It was at this point that Richard shut off the engine and began to return to the house, to give a message he had forgotten to pass on to his wife in the kitchen. Tim met him half-way:

'Mind if I have a go?'

'Richard was cautious, doubtful. 'Well, it takes a good deal of handling. It is a beast.'

'O, I'll be fine. I know my way around these things,' Tim was bright-eyed with enthusiasm.

'Well, all right…' Richard was not sure that this was going to be a happy partnership, but he acquiesced further. 'Remember, to slow down, you twist the grip towards you.'

'Have no fear!' Tim saluted his acknowledgment grinning unnervingly, and gleefully strode up the lawn to greet his new charge, Richard remembered.

Neil wondered casually if this enterprise would end well but thought better of articulating the question. Instead, he continued to sip Champagne.

The beast fired up first time giving Tim an extra boost of over-confidence. And off he went, quite steadily at first, then faster as his overconfidence knew no bounds.

Meanwhile, Richard discussed a culinary matter in the kitchen with his wife.

Neil watched impassively now as things seemed to be jogging along quite nicely. But, hang on a minute, the engine is beginning to race rather angrily. Ah, no, perhaps the wind simply caught the sound as the mower turned and all is well. Tim was now marching at the Grenadier Guards' pace, fastish, behind the mower, away from the Champagne terrace, parallel to and not far from the riverbank. (This conjures up a memory I have of the actor, Norman Wisdom, doing almost the same thing in one of his 1950s comedy films.) In fact, Tim was breaking into a trot. In a confused moment, Tim leaned heavily on the right side of the control bar and the machine lurched violently to the right, digging into the lawn, making a nice little seed drill all the way to the river. He also gave it a smart reminder of who's boss by pushing the throttle as far as he could, entirely the wrong way in the circumstances. The engine gave a long, agonised wail akin to the sound of a rising Harrier jump-jet as Tim let go and allowed the sorry machine to dive into the river where it splashed, spluttered a little and coughed its last.

Concurrently with this, Richard on hearing the distress of his beloved mower exclaimed to his wife: 'What the .... was that? It's bloody Hardy!' And at the same time, Neil rose in alarm and raced up the lawn to ensure no injury to the person had occurred, to find Tim stripping off his shoes and clothes and jumping into the river where only five or six burly men could have had any chance of rescuing the stricken mower.

Now, people began to gather. Richard and his wife had rushed from the kitchen and across the lawn. They stood for a few agonising seconds staring at the ridiculous sight of Tim's standing in the water feebly pawing at the mower looking as sheepish as a boy caught with his hand in the biscuit tin. The bereft owner of the mower threw aside any anger at the spectacle and he and his wife guffawed with uncontrolled mirth. Chortling, his wife raced for a camera and successfully caught that precious expression on Tim's face. With relief, Tim joined in the general fun.

Perhaps this is an amusing footnote. Michael Gambon, Tim's good friend, later added a caption to the photograph taken above. Michael is a master of dialect and of calligraphy. He beautifully penned on the mount of the framed photograph: 'Y'ere, where's my bloody grass to, my Zonnes?' Tim told me how the two of them were rather naughty during the Harry Potter films, giggling off camera and enjoying private jokes.

They worked well together, however, and in the Hagred's cottage scene when Fudge is trying to get his execution warrant signed quickly in *The Prisoner of Azkaban*, the two of them are actually 'ad libbing' much of that conversation. Of course, Dumbledore's procrastinations and insistence on setting down all his many Christian names, including Brian, enabled the two children to rescue that lovable animal, Buckbeak.)

PLUMBER 93.

*Yere where's the Bloody Grass too my*

# Tim and his Maker

'I believe Satan walks with very quiet shoes and very fast pace, all around us, all the time. But, by contrast, I also believe there is a God who will perhaps one day keep Satan in his place.'

So said Tim in a programme on BBC Radio 4, and this was quoted in the Order of Service booklet prepared for his memorial service on 25th October 2017 – St Crispin's Day. I had heard him say something similar at other times. They are curious words, but they envelop a common cry, perhaps. The evidence of Satan's work is all around us and, sometimes, we despair of the invisible God. This utterance was Tim's 'default' position, the very least of his belief. He, nonetheless, believed

183

in God unequivocally, and in his power. I did not quite agree with all these sentiments and once pointed out that Satan had already been vanquished by the Redeeming power of the death and Resurrection of Christ. Through our freedom of will we give new life and flesh to Satan in our weaknesses. Satan is usually right in front of us in a most attractive guise, Satan the great Obstructor. I ventured further, avoiding pietistic language. Satan was thus in the desert when tempting Christ and was there in St Peter as he attempted to persuade Christ that there was another way, other than sacrifice, to achieve God's purpose. That is why Peter was addressed harshly: 'Get thee behind me, Satan!'. Satan's task seems to be to obstruct our pathway to God, and we give him power when we acquiesce. If Satan is behind, he cannot obstruct. 'Somethin' in that, I s'pose.' Tim grinned, slipping easily into his mock cockney, and offered another gin, but undoubtedly thought further on the matter. There is wariness in the above quotation. Tim was wary, perhaps, of committing himself too far – beyond that which he could readily master and be confident in asserting and elucidating. Nevertheless, his belief in God was absolute. He would admit that God was revealed to us in Christ, though he would never attempt to explain the theology of the doctrine of the Holy Trinity. But he would fight his corner as battle-ready as any late medieval swordsman.

184

Tim had a dislike of atheists, particularly those he regarded as fanatical, like Professor Dawkins of Oxford. Tim so accused Dawkins in a fit of righteous indignation – what else? – at a university soirée, during a break in the proceedings, and had to be ushered gently away. 'They [scientists] are so absolutely bloody certain there is no Deity' he railed 'yet they cannot begin to understand how a bumble-bee is able to fly.' (I seem to remember, I might be wrong, that this was about 2010 when Dawkins was organizing an 'atheists' camp' for youth in opposition to the visit of His Holiness Pope Benedict XVI. In the event, I believe around 5,000 turned up at the Dawkins rally and hundreds of thousands cheered the Pope.)

There was in Tim a strong awareness of the spiritual, for the memories some buildings seem to hold; he, like the poet, Hopkins, could see the grandeur of God in Creation, and, in particular, the beauty of the countryside. He seemed to delight in the simple holy places: he was, for instance, strongly attracted to the four side chapels in the Oxford Oratory, and he was firmly convinced in the power of the sign of the cross, something he accepted without question. Perhaps he saw therein something of the 'sternness of God…e'en in the Crucifix' (*The Dream of Gerontius* – J H Newman). When he acted in anything for me, he always expressed his preference for the Oxford Oratory over many of the other venues.

Fr. Richard Duffield of the Oxford Oratory (now of the York Oratory): 'I was particularly privileged to 'work' with Robert when I introduced a fundraising evening at the Oxford Oratory. He was a delight to work with and absolutely professional in everything he did, a source of endless amusement and erudition on a plethora of subjects. For me, it was a thrill to be able to say that I had shared a stage with one of the greats!

Fr. Daniel Seward of the Oxford Oratory (now of the York Oratory): 'Despite international fame, starring in so many stellar roles, Robert Hardy was also happy to give his support to the Oxford Oratory on a number of occasions. He was Gerard Manley Hopkins and Brother Joseph in *Hildegard and Hopkins*, Tom the Shepherd in *The Herods* and Gerontius and the Soul in *The Dream of Gerontius*. He clearly gave these parts the same devotion and close attention as he did for his better-known parts, and was always gracious, unfussy, and always interested in the affairs of others. There is an Oratorian Priest who is still happy to exaggerate that he 'used to act with Robert Hardy' in consequence!'

Catholics and Protestants have always featured in Tim's family as in many, and he was at ease with either. Indeed, a great nephew is a Catholic monk in the north of Scotland, and Tim himself was practising Anglican, though an intermittent churchgoer. He was, of course, no modernist. I am convinced his private consideration of theological matters generally was more profound than he ever let slip. During his Scottish castle phase, he attended the local Episcopal church. He loved Evensong at Magdalen College, and often read a lesson at Evensong in Avington church, in the latter years of his life. He gave freely of his time annually at the service of nine lessons and carols at Christchurch Cathedral, Oxford, and innumerable other church functions. He confided that he felt closer to the Gospel truths when he played the character of Tom the Shepherd, I had written for him. And I think you could tell - but perhaps he was simply being kind to me. He certainly felt closer to understanding much of Catholic dogma that had worried him, when speaking John Henry Newman's words in the character of Gerontius. Certainly, I believe, something in the role of Gerontius raised his customary brilliant acting to an even higher plane. After his final performance in the role, he said: 'I like to think Newman had it about right.'

Towards the end of his life Tim once asked: 'What about the question of Transubstantiation, then?' He was serious but asked with a smile as though he was shy of being too serious. 'It is something I have never quite understood.' After giving him the appropriate definition, he said slowly: 'Yes, I see the logic in all of that.'

Tim certainly acted upon (not, of course, in any theatrical way!) many of the Christian principles he was brought up to adopt. He was generous with his time and gave freely of it to the young, to the fledgling actor, he gave valuable advice, and there was no end to the list of charitable organizations he supported in one way or another. And he knew who his neighbour was, (cf The Parable of the Good Samaritan) as the following account suggests even though it also reveals an unexpected naïveté. Tim's friend and neighbour, Charles Baker, wrote to me:

'I met Tim through the Mary Rose Trust. I ran an Archaeological Services company. Tim lived not far from me, near Oxford. We became friends and shared many happy times and much whisky! One story casts light on a facet of his character. My email account had been hacked and access gained to my contact list. The usual sort of scam resulted. My contacts were begged: 'Help, I have been mugged in Athens…' Money was asked for and almost immediately Tim sent the scammer £1,000 even after his bank and Western Union advised that this was likely to be a scam.' [Unfortunately, Tim failed first to ensure that Charles was not at his home in Oxfordshire!]

# Afterword

Well, have these sketches helped in securing the complete picture? Do we now have A Portrait of Robert Hardy recognizable to everyone? The outline was always there, of course, but his friends, acquaintances and family have added colour, nuance, subtlety, and, most of all, dimension. Has the colour and shading given us a trompe l'oeil effect? The third dimension gives us depth and the fourth, time, time to relive the stories and anecdotes we have been told, so we share the memories of all the contributors. Time to linger, as Tim stars again and again in these tales to the enquiring mind, the inquisitive and to those who just want to smile as often as possible. Has Tim left this world a better place for his ninety-one years sojourn? Despite his self-confessed faults, did his good qualities outweigh his flaws? A resounding yes is the answer to both questions.

Let's consider that our appreciation of history may well have been sharpened; better knowledge of the battlefields and the story of our forefathers' weaponry make matters clearer, perhaps. What was the cause and outcome of the battle of such and such, in the field over there? Who was our king then? What was the life of a longbowman like? What happened at Agincourt? How accurate was Shakespeare's account? How does the rescue of the *Mary Rose* expand our knowledge of Tudor England and the reign of Henry VIII? Light is thrown upon the answers to these questions from the illuminating work done by Tim over the years. Maybe, memories of a sketchy history lesson years ago, return, and, perhaps, begin to make sense. And, perhaps, the enquiring mind will seek further.

Has Tim's use of the English language both in the spoken and written word informed and instructed many? His performance of Shakespeare and poetry generally, was second to none. He understood the language perfectly, armed as he was with a background of Old and Middle English, particularly, Chaucer. He read poetry as though from the poet and never with that awful drawling 'poetry voice' so many affect when reading verse aloud.

And his acting has delighted and entertained in its infinite variety. Will viewers of *The Wilderness Years* not gain a better grasp of England just before the Second World War? Did his Prince Albert not help many understand better something of Victorian England? And all the time we were being entertained! Of course, not all his roles were instructive in that way, but with a glance through Tim's list of performances, one can see what good therapy they were and are for us. There was and is something for everyone.

Tim was BBC's first David Copperfield. He is still remembered for BBC's *An Age of Kings* by those old enough. He gave us a little of the ruthless in *The Troubleshooters* and his pugnacious chin was in evidence as Pontius Pilate in *Son of Man*. It was his Robert Dudly in *Elizabeth R* that so captivated Anne Curry, and many others. We see something of his gritty determination as an actor in Stephen Weeks's account of the filming of *Gawain and the Green Knight*. In *Edward VII* we saw his awkward relationship with Edward when the Prince of Wales, beautifully executed as was his stiff relationship with Donald (played by Neil) when he took the part of Sir Malcolm Campbell in *The Speed King*. As has been said so many times, his countless appearances as Churchill have moved his audiences profoundly. He was able to portray Churchill's depth of understanding, his determination and conviction, his vulnerability and petulance. In *The Shooting Party* he underplayed the character of Bob brilliantly and revealed a quietly pompous, insecure individual in sheer terror of losing his young wife to almost anyone around him. And then one comes across the outrageous comedy *Hot Metal* with Tim as the very funny but ridiculous character of Russell Spam. When I watched the programme after Tim's death, I realized how

191

much of Russell Spam he injected into our 'cockney' conversations.

And so, it goes on. What did the short-lived musical *Winnie* give us? If nothing else, it revealed Tim's light baritone of no mean quality. Then the long stint as Siegfried Farnon, a part for which he is, I suppose, best known. Peter Davison tells us a little of his experiences on the set with Tim. In many ways he was a good fit for the real vet he was impersonating as he was genuinely at ease with animals of all kinds.

In an episode of *Morse* he gave us his unpleasant tycoon with relish, and in *The Casebook of Sherlock Holmes* his Charles Augustus Milverton must be the most wonderfully repulsive portrayal of this character! He was pleased with his Mr Brooke in *Middlemarch* and with his Lord Rivers in *The Tichborne Claimant,* both memorable pieces of work.

He could be naughty on set - I earlier related the giggling incident when rehearsing *The Dream of Gerontius.* John Nettles *(Bergerac* and *Midsomer Murders)* disclosed that Tim so 'hammed up' his Robert Cavendish when mourning his murdered wife, that Tim and all the cast on set burst into rib-aching laughter. As the splendidly-judged Cornelius Fudge, Tim captures the anxious senior official perfectly. But Michael Gambon and Tim would find time to chuckle together between shots, off camera. In some respects he was simply a schoolboy

- and a mischievous one at that! Perhaps that is why he was so good with children and we have often seen in these pages.

Countless superb performances apart from those mentioned above - a good many of which are still available to us - I have not mentioned. Everyone will have his or her own happy memories. And many of Tim's fellow actors have provided thoughts, anecdotes and fun. Many, now dead, would have gladly put pen to paper, I am sure.

The lives Tim has touched and the smiles that have played over peoples' lips simply by casual acquaintance are innumerable. Those who have enjoyed a longer friendship know exactly what value they can place on that friendship. And we all may continue to enjoy our favourite episodes in his life either on film or by report or repute. I never saw Tim work on a length of yew wood with a draw-shave, but with the help of photographs supplied by generous contributors, I can now firmly believe I have watched him for hours on end!

TSRH

Requiescat In Pace

# Chronology

Timothy Sydney Robert Hardy born 29th October 1925

Rugby School

Magdalen College, Oxford [National Service in the RAF mid way]

Shakespeare Memorial Theatre - 1949 – 1951, various parts

West End Theatres - 1951 – 1953

Married Elizabeth Fox – 1952 (diss. 1956)

Old Vic: 1953–1954 USA – 1954-6 – 1958 (including Hamlet with Eileen Atkins and Henry V)

*David Copperfield* as David Copperfield, 1956 (Tim as BBC's first David Copperfield)

*Torpedo Run* as Lt. Redley, 1958, with Glen Ford and Ernest Borgnine

Shakespeare Memorial Theatre, 1959

*An Age of Kings* as Henry, Prince of Wales, 1960

*Rosmersholm* as Rosmer, 1960, The Comedy Theatre

Married Sally Pearson – 1961 (diss. 1986)

*The Rehearsal*, 1961, The Globe Theatre, with Maggie Smith

*A Question of Fact* as Colin Gardiner, 1962

*Picardy Affair*, writer, 1962

*The Spread of the Eagle* as Coriolanus, 1963

*A Severed Head* as Martin Lynch-Gibbon, 1963, The Criterion Theatre

*The Spy who came in from the Cold* as Dick Carlton, 1965

*The Troubleshooters* as Alec Stewart, 1966 – 1970

*The Baron (A Memory of Evil)* as Curt Hoffman, 1966

*How I won the War* as General, 1967

*Berserk* as Detective Superintendent Brooks, 1967

*The Constant Couple* as Sir Harry Wildair, 1967, New Theatre

*The Saint* as Walter Faber, 1968

*Son of Man* (The Wednesday Play) as Pontius Pilate, 1969

*I've Seen You Cut Lemons* as Robert Harmon, 1969, The Fortune Theatre

*Manhunt* as Sgt. Graz, 1969

*10 Rillington Place* as Malcolm Morris, 1971

*Elizabeth R* as Robert Dudley, 1971

*The Stalls of Barchester* as Doctor Haynes, 1971

*Young Winston* as Headmaster, 1972

*The Longbow* (writer), 1972

*Demons of the Mind* as Zom, 1972

*The Incredible Robert Baldick* as Sir Robert Baldick, 1972

*Psychomania* as C.I. Hesseltine, 1973

*Escape to Nowhere* as Assistant to the MI5 chief, 1973

*Gawain and the Green Knight* as Sir Bertilak, 1973

*Yellow Dog* as Alexander, 1973

*Dark Places* as Edward Foster, 1973

*The Gathering Storm* as von Ribbentrop, 1974

*The Slap* as Robert, 1974

*Habeas Corpus* as Dr Wicksteed, 1974, Lyric Theatre

*Edward VII* as The Prince Consort, 1975 [With his moustache, Tim was able to grasp that delightfully haughty nineteenth-century-look and it was captured perfectly by Joy Stanley Ricketts in her portrait of Tim as the Prince Consort, mounted on the fine horse Magic Lantern. (I believe that attractive animal starred in *National Velvet*.) I am now fortunate enough to own that painting and I pass it every time I climb the stairs.]

*Upstairs Downstairs*, Episode 'Such a Lovely Man' as Sir Guy Paynter, 1975

*The Duchess of Duke Street* as George Duggan, 1976

*Longbow – A Social and Military History* (book), 1976 ff

*Horses in our Blood* (writer), 1977

*All Creatures Great and Small* as Siegfried Farnon, 1978-1980, 1983, 1985, 1987-1990

Mary Rose Trust (Consultant) 1979 ff (Trustee) 1991 ff

*Twelfth Night* as Sir Toby Belch, 1980

*The Pied Piper of Hamelin* (Narrator), 1980

Appointed Commander of the Order of the British Empire (CBE), 1981

*Speed King* as Malcolm Campbell, 1981

*Fothergill* as John Fothergill, 1981

*The Wilderness Years* as Churchill, 1981

Member of Co. of Woodmen of Arden – 1981 ff

*Dear Liar*, 1982, Mermaid Theatre

*Gordon of Khartoum* (writer), 1982

*The Far Pavilions* as The Commandant, 1983

WWF (Trustee), 1983 – 1989

Board of Trustees of the Royal Armouries, 1984 – 1995

Battlefields Panel, English Heritage, 1984 ff

Berkshire, Buckingham, Oxfordshire Naturalists' Trust Appeal, 1984 -1990

*The Zany Adventures of Robin Hood* as King Richard, 1984

*The Shooting Party* as Lord Bob Lilburn, 1985

*Jenny's War* as Klein, 1985

*Make or Break* as John Garrard, 1986

*Paying Guests*, 1986

*Churchill in the USA*, 1986

*Hot Metal* as Twiggy Rathbone and Russell Spam, 1986-8

*Northanger Abbey* as General Tilney, 1987

Court of the Worshipful Co. of Bowyers 1988-1990

*Paris by Night* as Adam Gillvray, 1988

*Marcus Welby in Paris* as Dr Price – 1988

*War and Remembrance* as Churchill, 1988

*Winnie* as Churchill, 1988

*Bomber Harris* as Churchill, 1989

Awarded Hon. D.Litt – Reading University 1990

*The Casebook of Sherlock Holmes* as Charles Augustus Milverton, 1992

*Body and Soul,* Albery Theatre, 1992

*Inspector Morse* (Episode 'Twilight of the Gods') as Andrew Baydon, 1993

*Middlemarch* as Mr Brooke, 1994

*Mary Shelley's Frankenstein* as Professor Krempe, 1994

The move from Upper Bolney, Henley-on-Thames to the Scottish Castle - Newhall

*A Feast at Midnight* as The Headmaster, 1995

*Sense and Sensibility* as Sir John Middleton, 1995

*Gulliver's Travels* as Dr Parnell, 1996

*Bramwell* as Sir Herbert Hamilton, 1996

Admitted Fellow of Society of Antiquaries (FSA) – 1996

Awarded Hon. D.Litt – Durham University – 1997

*Mrs Dalloway* as Sir William Bradshaw, 1997

*Castle Ghosts of England, Scotland, Wales, and Ireland,* narrator and interviewer, 1997

The move from Newhall to Charlbury, Oxfordshire

*Nancherrow* as Viscount Berryan, 1998

*The Tichborne Claimant* as Lord Rivers, 1998

*The Barber of Siberia* as Forsten, 1998

*An Ideal Husband* as Lord Caversham, 1998

*Midsomer Murders* as Robert Cavendish, 1999

*Celui qui a dit non* as Churchill, 1999

*Justice in Wonderland* as Mr Justice Morland, 2000

*The Lost World* as Professor Illingworth, 2001

*Foyle's War* as Henry Beaumont – 2001

*Thunderpants* as The Doctor, 2002

*The Gathering* as The Bishop, 2002

*Bertie and Elizabeth* as Roosevelt, 2002

*The Falklands Play* as HM Ambassador to the United Nations, 2002

*Harry Potter and the Chamber of Secrets* as Cornelius Fudge, Minister for Magic, 2002

*Lucky Jim* as Professor Neddy Welch, 2003

*Spooks* as Governor of the Bank of England, 2003

*Harry Potter and the Prisoner of Azkaban* as Cornelius Fudge, Minister for Magic, 2004

*Making Waves* as Father Parry, 2004

*Harry Potter and the Goblet of Fire* as Cornelius Fudge, Minister for Magic, 2005

*Lassie* as Judge Murray, 2005

*The Herods* as Tom the Shepherd, 2005

*The Great Warbow (from Hastings to the Mary Rose)* (book, written with co-author Matthew Strickland), 2006

*The Herods* as Tom the Shepherd, 2006

*Agatha Christie's Marple* as Churchill, 2006

*Master and Commander* series Patrick O'Brian (Audio) – 2006 ff

*Harry Potter and the Order of the Phoenix* as Cornelius Fudge, Minister for Magic, 2007

*Hildegard and Hopkins* as Hopkins and Br. Joseph, 2007

*Framed* as Provost, 2008

*Little Dorrit* as Tite Barnacle Senior, 2008

*Gerontius* as Gerontius, Beaulieu Abbey, 2008

*Margaret* as William Whitelaw, 2009

*Old Harry* as Harry, 2009

*Gerontius* as Gerontius, Oxford Oratory, Oxford Cathedral, 2009

*Lewis* as Professor of Music, 2010

*Rumpole of the Bailey* (Audio) 2010

Battlefields Trust (Patron) 2010 ff

*Gerontius* as Gerontius, Winchester Cathedral, 2011

Battlefields Trust President 2011 ff

*The Audience* as Churchill, Gielgud Theatre, 2013

The move from Charlbury to Avington

*Churchill: 100 days that saved Britain* as Churchill, 2015

*Joseph's Reel* as Joseph, 2015

*Snapshot Wedding* as Donald, 2017

*In Familia* as Sir Ashton Leonard, 2017

Death – 3rd August 2017

This list does, of course, not include the readings, lectures, and speeches he gave here, there, and everywhere. Nor does it include the Churchill letters he read before large audiences along with Celia Sandys, who read from Clemmie's letters. It does not include all those countless occasions when he was prevailed upon to talk of the longbow, this battlefield or that, the Mary Rose, or to talk about or be his beloved Churchill.

# Acknowledgments

I place in alphabetical order all those who have assisted me by giving me tales and anecdotes. If I have omitted anyone who ought to appear, incompetence on my part is to blame rather that ingratitude.

Eileen Atkins, David Austin, Charles Barker, Sarah Bullen, Henry Lytton Cobbold, Giovanna Cresswell-Forrester, Anne Curry, Peter Davison, Judi Dench, Carol Drinkwater, Lesley Duff, Fr Richard Duffield, Martin Marix Evans, Julian Fellowes, John Selwyn Gilbert, Clive Hallum- Baker, Emma Hardy, Henry Hardy, Justine Hardy, Paul Hardy, Nigel Havers, Alex Hildred, Douglas Hodge, Ang Lee, Robert Lindsay, Michael Linnit, John Lippiat, Chris May, Colin Meays, Alistair Miles, Ralph Montagu, Charles Montgomery, James Murray, Neil Nisbet (Robertson), Terri Palmer, Sarah Parish, Geoff Pope, Richard Prideaux-Brune, Neil Robertson (Nisbet), Sinclair Rogers, Nick Rule, Celia Sandys, Fr Daniel Seward, Howard Simmons, Matthew Strickland, Nina Sosanya, Sarah Vey, Stephen Weeks, Greg Wilson.

Among the organizations ready to assist were The Mary Rose Trust, The Battlefields Trust and the Tewkesbury Battlefield Society. And it is the Battlefields Trust I must thank for permission to reproduce 'The Battle of Homildon Hill' which first appeared in 'Battlefield' the journal of that Trust.

Special thanks is due to all those who supplied me with their photographs and snapshots with no strings attached, and to Ralph Montagu and the Radio Times, the BBC photo-library and the ITV agents, Shutterstock for granting licences to use their property. Thanks also to the Newhall Estate allowing me to use photos taken by Tigerchick. I have endeavoured to identify ownership of everything passed to me and I apologize if any item has slipped through the net.

Thanks to Auriel Roe of Dogberry Books who edited with much patience.

Although listed above and apparent from the book, I am indebted to Tim's family and to Neil for their forbearance.

It is my hope that the charities – of great interest to Tim – Healing Kashmir, The Murray Parish Trust and the Oxford Oratory will benefit from the publication of this work.

JC-M

Julien Chilcott-Monk founded and directs the choirs Vox Humana and Gregoriana. His dramatizations of works by Evelyn Waugh, Gerard Manley Hopkins and Medieval writers have been staged in major venues throughout the UK. As an author, he is known for *A Calendar of Catholic Devotion* and *Week by Week with St John Henry Newman* among other titles. *Call me Tim,* a celebration of the life of Julien's friend, the actor and historian Robert Hardy, is something of a departure but the author believes there may yet be a comic novel to be written. He lives with his wife and a twenty-year-old dove, the last of a flight of thirty, in Winchester.

from the Minister
for Magic

and

Robert Hardie

Printed in Great Britain
by Amazon

17891270R00122